A STUDY ON PRENATAL STRESS AND DEVELOPMENT OF PREGNANCY STRESS SCALE

SREEJA GANGADHARAN. P.

ACKNOWLEDGEMENT

It is often a blessing to have a mentor who has the wisdom and the right vision about the future of his mentees. I had the privilege and honour to pursue my Ph. D research under the guidance and direction of such a mentor, Prof. SPK Jena. I express my deep and sincere gratitude to him for the constant, motivation and freedom for doing innovative research. I would like to extend my cordial thanks to Prof. Chadha, Prof. Nandita Babu, Prof. Anand Prakash (who were in charge as the head of the department during the period of my Ph D) for providing the necessary facilities to carry out my research work.

I would like to thank all the staff members in the Obstetrics and Gynecology department of St Stephen's and Tirath Ram Shah hospital who gave me the permission and extended all the support to conduct my study at their premises. I would like to extend my cordial thanks to my former guide and supervisors Dr. Anita Srivastava and Dr. Priya Bir, and all the members in the Ph.D. advisory committee. I would like to thank all my professors and mentors who had sparked the quest for research in me which made to dedicate my five years to this.

I would like to express my sincere gratitude to my mother who is my constant moral support and encouragement in all my endeavours, without which this thesis would not have been possible. Thank you, Mom. I would like to thank my Dad, for his constant moral and financial support in all my difficult phases of this research and in my life. I also extend my sincere thanks to my sisters for their love and care which gave me confidence throughout this phase of ups and downs. I am also grateful to all technical and nontechnical staffs in the department who did all the paper work for me at the backend.

Last, but not the least, I thank almighty, for his constant support and companionship through all my miseries and for showing me the way ahead where I find no road ahead.

(Sreeja Gangadharan P)

TABLE OF CONTENTS

CERTIFICATE ii
DECLARATION iii
ACKNOWLEDGEMENTS iv
ABSTRACT v

Introduction 1
    Pregnancy and Transition to Motherhood 1
    Conceptualising Prenatal Maternal Stress 4
    Risks associated with Prenatal Maternal Stress 5
    Concerns during Pregnancy / Sources of Prenatal Stress 5
    Various Approaches in Stress Research 12
    Assessment of Prenatal Maternal Stress 13

Literature Review 17
    Prenatal Stress 17
    Theoretical Framework 19
    Stress and Depression during Pregnancy 21
    Strains in intimate partner relation 23
    Poor social support/ interpersonal relation 24
    Infanticide or foeticide 25
    Incidence of pregnancy loss 26
    Prenatal stress and health compromising behavior 26
    Pregnancy Specific Stress measure 28
    Summary 40
    Objectives 41

Method 42
    Phase 1:   Development of Items and Content Validity Assessment by Subject Matter Experts 42
    Phase 2:   Standardization of the Scale 46

Results and Discussion **53**

Phase 1: **53**

    Content validity assessment 53

    Instrument design 59

Phase 2: **60**

    Reliability 64

    Validity 64

    Factor analysis 66

    Follow-up model testing using confirmatory factor analysis 70

    Factor description and discussion 72

Summary and Conclusion **78**

    Limitations of the present study and Suggestions for future research 79

    Implications of the study 80

Conclusion **81**

References **82**

Appendices **100**

Appendix A 100

Appendix B 103

LIST OF TABLES

	Description	Page No
Table 1	Pregnancy Specific Stress Measures	39
Table 2	Demographic details of the sample interviewed	53
Table 3	Code and related themes	54
Table 4	I-CVI and CVR for initial 40 items	57
Table 5	Demographic details of the sample considered in the Phase 2: Pilot study	60
Table 6	Demographic details of the sample considered in the Phase 2: N= 356	61
Table 7	Descriptive Statistics of the initial 31 item scale	62
Table 8	Mean and item–total correlation of 31 items PNMSS (N = 356)	63
Table 9	Demographic details of the 60 samples considered for test retest reliability	64
Table 10	Test-retest reliability statistics of 31items on 60 pregnant women	65
Table 11	Eigen Values of Exploratory Factor Analysis	67
Table 12	Factor Loadings of items on Exploratory Factor Analysis	68
Table 13	Eigen Values of Exploratory Factor Analysis	69
Table 14	CFI, TLI and RMSEA of the two models using Confirmatory Factor Analysis	70
Table 15	Mean, Standard Deviation of the four sub groups on the sub dimension, Perceived Social Support and Preparedness	73
Table 16	Mean, Standard Deviation of the four sub groups on the sub dimension, Pregnancy Specific Concerns	73
Table 17	Mean, Standard Deviation of the four sub groups on the sub dimension, Intimate Partner Relation	74
Table 18	Mean, Standard Deviation of the four sub groups on the sub dimension Economic Concerns	75
Table 19	Mean, Standard Deviation of the sample on four sub dimensions, entire scale and the four sub groups	75

LIST OF FIGURES

	Description	Page Number
Figure 1	Theoretical conceptualisation of prenatal stress	21
Figure 2	Thematic map	55
Figure 3	Thematic flowchart	56
Figure 4	Scree Plot	57
Figure 5	Four factor model – CFA	71

Introduction

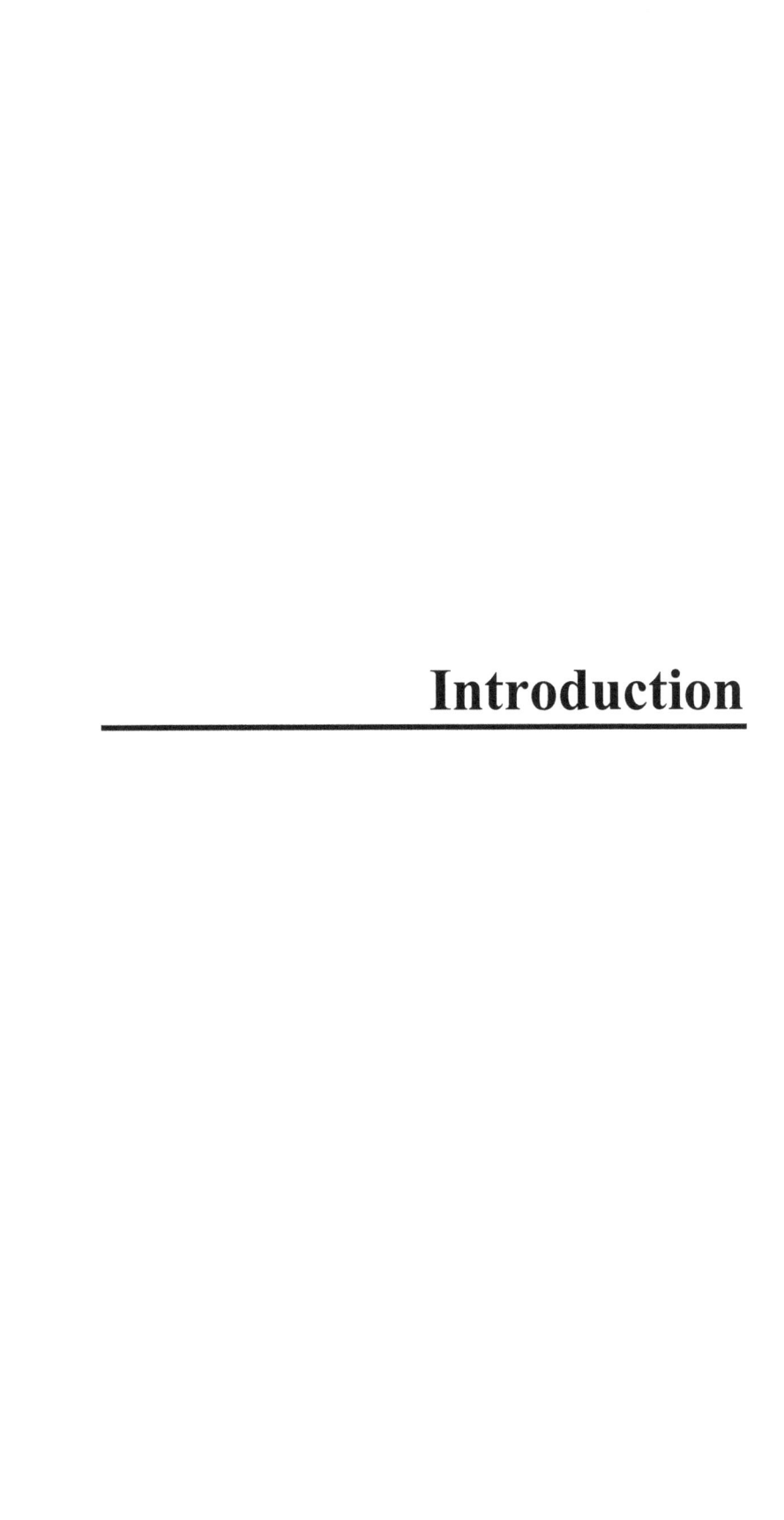

A Study on Prenatal Stress and Development of Pregnancy Stress Scale

Pregnancy, though being a state associated with extreme joy and happiness, it is also a period of physical and emotional transition in women. Since reproductive events are associated with substantial hormonal changes and subsequent mood swings, some may perceive it as stressful if aligned with other adverse environment. This makes her extremely vulnerable psychologically and biologically to the repercussions and they may experience a heightened amount of stress and depression during his period (Weinstock, 2008; Weerth & Buitelaar, 2005).

Pregnancy is described in the psychoanalytic literature as "…. a period of crisis involving profound psychological as well as somatic changes." (Bibring, 1959). Psychoanalysts describes a particular dynamics during this phase; involving a psychological crisis and a process of maturation arising from the experience of a new developmental phase: 'Parenthood'. This period of crisis may compromises health and wellbeing of young mother and put them under immense stress which may leads to depression, if not managed properly.

In addition to this intra psychic conflict, medical research suggests that multiple adaptations of women's neuroendocrine systems during pregnancy makes them vulnerable to mood disorder, both in pregnancy and in postpartum period (Brunton & Russel, 2008). Hence from a holistic perspective, maternity care should encompass both physiological and psychological aspects of pregnant women.

This chapter presents an overview of various concerns women have during their pregnancy, their experiences and commonly used measures to assess stress among pregnant women along with it's limitations. The chapter also gives a glimpse of physiological aspects of prenatal stress along with its potential risks on foetal neural development and adverse birth outcomes such as preterm delivery, low birth weight and other neurodevelopmental issues.

Pregnancy and Transition to Motherhood

Pregnancy or gestation that occurs by sexual intercourse or by assisted reproductive technology is a state during which women carries a foetus in uterus (NICHD, 2013). Pregnancy lasts around 40 weeks and ends with childbirth. Although the average duration of pregnancy is 39- 40 weeks, pregnancy is typically divided into three stages or trimesters. The total duration is 42 weeks and each trimester is defined as period of 14 weeks. The experience of women in each of these trimesters varies, and this needs a brief description.

No matter how well a woman is prepared for her pregnancy, the first trimester is a period of constant irritants for many. Many symptoms and discomforts of pregnancy (Campbell & Klocke, 2001) are entirely normal, including cardiovascular, hematologic, metabolic, renal, and respiratory changes and don't significantly interfere with activities of daily life or pose a threat to the health of the baby or the mother unless she is exposed to any intrauterine risks.

As compared to the first trimester women experience mood swings less frequently in the second trimester. This period of pregnancy, which spans from 13 to 27 week is called 'honeymoon' period and is a wonderful experience for the woman. From here onwards she starts experiencing her pregnancy more physically and mentally. The movements she starts feeling by the 16th week of her pregnancy are called 'quickening'. The discomfort she felt during the initial weeks of this trimester starts disappearing as the baby grows within her.

Depression is far less frequent, but she may experience an increased worry (Bennet, Einarson, Taddio, Koren & Einarson, 2005) about her pregnancy during this stage. Any negative memories about her past pregnancy (Bergner, Beyer, Klapp & Rauchfuss, 2008) or ongoing marital problems may contribute to depression (Glover, 2011). Changes in her appearance due to weight gain may disappoint her and needs constant reassurance form partner about her looks.

The tiredness she felt during the early stage of her pregnancy returns with the onset of third trimester. The body feels more heavy and stressed. Everything from getting out of bed, standing up from a chair needs extra effort. She may completely lose her sex drive partly due to her physical changes and partly due to her focus on labour, delivery and parenthood. Lack of complete understanding of these emotional and physical changes of the partner, what they are undergoing during the pregnancy, may leads to stress and depression and may persist as postnatal depression.

During her third trimester, she experiences more quickening which brings her more emotionally closer to the unborn child. Her nesting instincts may make her feel the need to prepare the house to bring the baby home. She also experience increased physical discomfort such as aching back, pelvis, and hips, tingling and numbness, puffiness, abdominal pain, shortness of breath, swollen limbs, varicose veins etc. (Campbell & Klocke, 2001). Women who are lacking physical and emotional support from their family and/or intimate partner may find it extremely difficult to cope with these.

Pregnant women experience a heightened fear and anxiety as she approaches her labour and delivery (Redshaw, Martin, Rowe & Hockley, 2009). Primigravida, the first time mothers experience higher stress as compared to multigravida. She will be more stressed if she had any history of prenatal loss (Armstrong, 2004; Bergner et al., 2008) or any medical risks or other co-morbidities in this pregnancy (Yali & Lobel, 1999).

While coming to parenthood, pregnancy is the first stage of transition to motherhood in women's and fatherhood in men's life. The role of a mother and a father is obviously viewed with tonnes of responsibilities and sacrifices. This is the second step in building a family, hence for some it is a blessing and for others it is often an unwelcoming surprise. Hence approach of each couple; to each of their pregnancy may vary despite the ideal notion that pregnancy always brings positive emotions, joy and celebrations.

Those couples who had least prepared for the event, may experience a little embarrassment and confusion. Hence their first step to parenthood is to accept the fact of being pregnant and assimilating it to one's way of living. But the degree of acceptance at any time depends on one's readiness and level of preparedness and support they receive from their intimate partner.

Women's attitude towards her pregnancy could be acceptance, satisfaction, pride, rejection or ambivalence. Attitude of her spouse and his care and attention to their pregnancy influences her approach to it as an illness, a mere physical or medical condition or an event that is supposed to add more joy and meaning to their life. Negative attitudes results from considering pregnancy as an event, often unattractive, vulnerable, uncomfortable and depending on others may affect her self-attitude and is likely to produce irritability and increased anxiety and depression.

For some women realisation of responsibilities could trigger a sense of fear and this may be aggravated by unfavourable conditions which may results in unresolved conflicts with motherhood (Bobak, Lowdermilk, & Jensen, 1995). Though many women experience an ambivalence, increased body sensation, feeling of dependence etc. during pregnancy, those who considers pregnancy as a positive event experiences psychological and biological fulfilment, increased self-esteem and tend to be more confident about the outcome and may not always perceives the events associated with pregnancy as stressful.

Conceptualising Prenatal Maternal Stress

Women enters a complex world once they become pregnant; they experience a series of concerns from physiological and emotional transition including: changes in appearance, changes in interpersonal relations, labour and delivery, parenting, health of the foetus and fear of medical complications (Lobel, 1998; Dunkel Schetter, 2011), which often requires an increased physiological as well as psychological resources to cope efficiently.

Her emotional attachment to the unborn baby demands her to take additional care on her own wellbeing (Rowe & Fisher, 2010) as well as her pregnancy. While majority of women adapt successfully to pregnancy and motherhood, some may find their everyday life as extremely challenging and difficult to manage and to them, childbearing years becomes a perfect storm and my leads to major depressive disorders (MDD).

Lobel and colleagues (Lobel & Dunkel-Schetter, 1990), used a multidimensional approach to define Prenatal Maternal Stress (PNMS) based on foundational work of Lazarus on stress suggesting it as a combination of stressful events or conditions ("stressors"), perceptions or evaluations of these stressors ("appraisals"), and stress responses such as emotions (Lazarus & Folkman., 1984). This multidimensional framework was used by latter studies to explore various spheres of prenatal maternal stress.

Most of the women experience a spectrum of psychiatric symptoms such as anxiety and depression around the child bearing and puerperal period (Zuckerman, Amaro, Bauchner & Cabral, 1989). These symptoms may occur both during and following pregnancy and if not treated, it may persists and go beyond the normative, into pathological experiences. These may often leads to undesirable consequences such as compromised mental health, difficulty in maternal role development, poor quality of life, ability to function, quality of relationships and social engagement (Emmanuel & St John, 2010). The extent of this may depends on the level of maternal distress and support system available to them.

Studies shows that approximately one in every ten women have major to minor depression during pregnancy or in the postpartum period. Women in their childbearing years accounts for the largest population of Americans with depression. Stress during pregnancy is the most common complication and the major risk factor for postpartum depression (ACOG, 2006). Depression during pregnancy and/or in the postpartum period occurs approximately among 10- 15% of women (Bennett et al., 2005; Deitz, Homa, England, Berly, Tong & Dube, 2010).

Risks associated with Prenatal Maternal Stress

Earlier studies had identified prenatal maternal stress as an intrauterine environment risk for foetal neural development (Drunkel-Schetter, 2011) and adverse birth outcomes like preterm delivery and low birth weight (Copper Goldenberg, Swain, & Norman 1996; Dole, Savitz, Siega-Riz, Hertz-Picciotto, Mcmahon, & Buekens 2004). Such adverse birth outcomes are the leading cause for infant mortality, morbidity and other health problems that may persist into childhood, adolescence and even adulthood.

Prenatal maternal stress, anxiety, and depression could have a programming effect on foetus if the pregnant woman is subjected to prolonged exposure to stress hormones, this could adversely affect the foetal neural development (Alder, Fink, Bitzer, Hosli, & Holzgreve, 2007). Many prospective and retrospective studies have conducted in this line, which had contributed to a huge literature supporting this foetal programming hypothesis (Huizink, Mulder & Buitelaar, 2004; Mulder, Robles de Medina, Huisink, Van den Bergh, Bmtelaar & Visser, 2002; Talge, Neal, & Glover, 2007).

Concerns during Pregnancy / Sources of Prenatal Stress

Beliefs, values and attitudes. Rearing and racing child is one of the duty nature assigned to women and the society also shapes her believes in similar line. If she thinks, she failed in this duty to give full care and dedication to her pregnancy or consider an abortion; either for career, or due to her medical conditions or any other factor even external to her control, she tends to blame herself for her omissions and internalises such failures. This will further bring down her self- worth which she associates herself with women-hood.

Society views motherhood as a criterion for womanhood and her decision to remain child free could be stigmatized as a deviant or unnatural behaviour. Hence one's decision regarding pregnancy is framed by personal values on the meaning and importance of motherhood as well as the societal values and familial pressure. At times, women may succumb to such pressures and become pregnant even though they were not mentally prepared for it.

Changing circumstances and increasing opportunities to explore untouched arenas had helped her to explore more potential either in her career or in her passion, outside the home. This helped her to explore more arenas which were strange and unfamiliar to her. This gradually brings down the importance, women associate herself with motherhood as an essential criterion for womanhood, self satisfaction and self esteem (MC Quillan, Greil, Shreffler, & Tichenor, 2008). Some studies says, religious exposure in the early life appears to influence later child bearing decisions among women (Pearce, 2002) and lower level of religiosity in adulthood is associated with being voluntarily childless (Abma & Martinez, 2006).

Planning and preparedness. Level of preparedness is the most important factor in accepting the role and taking the responsibly in parenting. In the case of unwanted pregnancy it is essential for the couples to consider a decision regarding the continual of their pregnancy or to resolve the career related issues or any other concerns, at an early stage of pregnancy itself.

Pregnancies are not a positive event for all (Geller, 2004) and a positive pregnancy outcome may not occur for all women or for all pregnancies, hence at times they are required to make decisions regarding termination of an unwanted pregnancy, but, this also includes certain legal restrictions. If these couple find it difficult to accept their pregnancy and assimilate it to their life, they will left with the only option of abortion. Induced abortions (voluntary termination of pregnancy) may be either therapeutic (where decision centres on the health of the mother or the foetus) or elective (voluntary termination due to any other reason) is emotionally taxing for the mother and should be handled with at most care and sensitivity by the health care professionals and intimate partner. Under such circumstances; where women required to take decision regarding their pregnancy, they may tend to delay the decisions either due to fear or anxiety. At times she may experience ambivalence even if she recognizes her reasons to continue their pregnancy (Kirkman, Rowe, Hardiman, Mallett & Rosenthal, 2009).

Period before conception is very important for physical and mental health and wellbeing of pregnant women. Poor preconception care may even contribute to maternal death and babies with genetic abnormalities (Ben –Shlomo & Kuh, 2002; Hansen, Slagsvold & Moum, 2009). Hence, preconception planning and preparedness constitute an important component of prenatal care.

Previous pregnancy loss. Women who had experienced a pregnancy loss; referred as foetal mortality, an intrauterine death of the foetus at any gestational age (Mac Dorman & Kirmeyer 2009), may experience depression for a brief period and a heightened maternal anxiety during her subsequent pregnancies (Armstrong, 2004; Bergner et al., 2008). In induced abortions due to medical conditions women may often tries to rationalize her decision but in elective abortion they may face more ambivalence and results in post-abortion syndrome, a traumatic emotional reaction that persists months after such abortion. Post abortion distress may be experienced mostly by women at a younger age and primigravidas.

Technology assisted pregnancy. Infertility is a major condition under which women seeks to become pregnant with the assistance of Artificial Reproductive Technique (ART). The most common and the effective ART is In Vitro Fertilization (IVF), but with the use of such external assistance, women may experience fear and anxiety about the foetus and for her own health during the entire span of pregnancy.

Those women who had received infertility treatment may often experience mood swings caused by hormonal treatments. They also faces social challenges and perceived stigma attributed to their infertility as a personal failure. Hence decisions regarding reproductive health events could be quite stressful for such couples and includes significant emotional responses, which has to be addressed by the health care professionals.

Late pregnancy. With greater societal changes and diversity of life choices either in terms of partner or in terms of career, women delays childbearing into later reproductive years. This is particularly seen in those with greater educational qualification, higher career aspirations and work experience and those having higher socioeconomic status (Livingston & Cohen, 2010). There are myriads of reasons why women delay pregnancy: establishing a career or finding a suitable mate, were few. Fertility declines by age and women with 35 years or older are classified as advanced maternal age and are considered as "high risk" category by gynaecologists. Such high risk pregnancies are stressful for the expecting mothers during the entire span of their pregnancy.

Second time mother or multigravidas. The family environment and concerns are a little different for a multigravida. One of her major concern is the age, personality and health of the first child. Due to the lack of resources mother's capacity for empathy with the first child is under stress during this period. The child may engage in more regressive or babyish ways to express his/ her distress where as the mother expect them to act like a mature older sibling. This may often results in a collapse of their cherished closeness and could give rise to an overpowering sense of guilt in the mother (Gottlieb & Mendelson, 1995).

Interpersonal relation. Social support is an exchange of emotional and material resources to an individual which is intended to promote health and wellbeing of the recipient. Social support reduces stress by altering the perception of threat, lowering anxiety (Stanton, Lobel, Sears & DeLuca, 2002; Moak & Agrawal, 2010) and by improving one's coping abilities. Studies found that women with good social support have significantly lower stress as compared to women with poor social support (Aranda, Castaneda, Lee & Sobel, 2001). Support by spouse, a reliable family member or a friend before, during and/or after the pregnancy helps to improve foetal as well as the mother's health significantly (Aranda et al., 2001).

Mother – daughter relation. The reaction of mother to her daughter's pregnancy should be respect for her anatomy, helping the young women to adapt to her pregnancy and later motherhood (Boback et al., 1995). The daughter may have difficulty to accept her identity with her own mother; hence the mother could lend her a helping hand to handle this.

If there were any constrains in their relationship, the young women may consider every offer of help or advice as a hostile gesture and may compromise the emotional support and physical care that may arises out of a good, healthy relation. To avoid this, the daughter should accept her mother before judging what kind of mother she is, and what kind of relationship they had.

Relationship with intimate partner. Gender expectations encourage women to value relatedness and nurturance of others. A woman has to enact her ability for nurturance, in many sphere of her relationship; this may help her to fulfil various roles in her life such as a loving partner, caring mother, obedient daughter etc. This ideals of femininity extends to the area of sexuality in which women puts the needs of her partner and engages in sexual care taking of the partner's need with less attention to one's own sexual desire or lack of desire. Hence during pregnancy, her inability to meet the sexual desires of her spouse due to her physical and emotional changes may put her under stress.

On the other hand, the cultural expectations of appropriate behaviour could influence the response of a male partner to his female partner's needs during their pregnancy. Bobak and Jensen (1995) reported that, for a woman, two major needs from her spouse during their pregnancy are: the first is the need for love and value, the second is acceptance of the child and his willingness to assimilate the infant to the family.

During the whole process of pregnancy, the couple gets closer and this has a maturing effect on their relationship. While they assume new roles they discover new aspects of each other, those who trust and support each other shares a mutual dependence on needs. Father-to-be is seen as a source of physical and emotional support and who cares and nurtures the partner and stays besides her during difficulties. Since she being engrossed in thoughts of unborn child, the partner may at times feel "left out". Hence the emotions experienced by the male partner also vary during pregnancy. Some may engage in nurturing behaviour while others may feel lonely and alienated; they may seek comfort and understanding from outside world, others may engage in new hobbies or preoccupied with their own emotional developments and often fails to become the emotional support she needs. This may results in perpetual miseries and unwanted strains in their relationship.

Intimate partner violence is a major concern that prevails across culture. According to the study by International Centre for Research on Women, conducted among 9000 men in India, 60% of men interviewed had admitted of perpetrating at least one or the other form of intimate partner violence- ranging from emotional or economic torture to physical or sexual violence. It is extremely stressful and may bring pathological consequences, if women were exposed to such emotional, physical and economic abuses from the intimate partner, especially during her pregnancy.

A recent reports brought out by the Family Planning Associate of India (FPAI), has marked a rise in the number of pregnancies terminated by married women over years. The report further states that, this trend is not just due to financial burden, but due to the fact that many women gets pregnant by accident and without their consent. Experts add that most married women who were abused in such manner ends up in chronic depression and trauma.

Studies show that, women who are nurtured by her male partner have less emotional and physical symptoms, labour and child birth complications and easier postpartum adjustments (Aarts & Vingerhoets, 1993; Reece, 1993). A satisfying physical and emotional bonding is one of the major joy in a marital relationship and women who are satisfied in their sexual life are tends to report greater wellbeing (Davision, Bell, La China, Holden & Davis, 2009).

Mother-child bonding. A mother's relationship with her child could be seen as a physiological, psychological and emotional whole. From the moment the women came to know that she is pregnant, she is in the process of becoming a mother. The relationship with the unborn child, which had begun from conception, further extends and strengthens through pregnancy, birth, feeding and care. During the journey, she attains emotional maturity, tolerance, ability to withstand pain through various sacrifices which she had committed for the sake of having a child.

Psychological adaptation to pregnancy varies with the course of pregnancy. The intensive physiological changes during the first three months such as nausea, dizziness, vomiting, head ache and appetite disturbances may cause intense psychological pressure and distress. Many find it difficult to cope with such stressors and this reflects in either emotional or physical consequences. After the initial irritants during the first few months of her pregnancy, she may be in a fantasy about her expecting child, and gets frustrated if her fantasies didn't turned out to be a reality.

By the second trimester, women withdraw herself and starts experiencing her pregnancy (Cambell & Field, 1989) more physically and emotionally and may engrossed in the thoughts of unborn child. She may experience constant mood swings.

Various factors stands on her way and the most common is the fear of losing her personality in favour of her child which may manifest itself as a primitive fear of death or concern over physical beauty (Affonso & Mayberry, 1990; Chen, Chen and Huang, 1989). It may be an oppressed fear for obligations and restrictions associated with pregnancy or from the frustrations out of professional and intellectual compromises. Only those families having a healthy emotional bonding could overcome such concerns.

The emotional intensities and reactions to pregnancy related events may vary drastically since it's inseparably connected to one's personality. Many women may have highly motivated to experience motherhood, but others apparently have not considered it in any detail. Women, who are internally and externally deprived of love may have difficulty in expressing love and compassion and may be accompanied by a spiteful neglect of parental care.

By creating a good emotional bond with the partner during this time, the couple could build the foundation for a healthy family life and could improve emotional bonding with their unborn child. In the last three months women experiences an increased fear and anxiety, and it appears to be somewhat an approach- avoidance conflict about delivery.

Labour and delivery. During the last week of pregnancy; there arises a conflict between the will to expel and the will to retain, both of these are considered as pathological characters. If the expulsive forces win an upper hand the results may be a premature delivery on the other hand if one fears to assume the responsibility, tends to have prolonged pregnancy. Such abnormal and persistent fear of child birth is known as Tokophobia. Those long hours of contraction represents a crisis which brings her closer to the deepest and the most intense physical sensation and emotional stressor. The pain, fear, exertion, doubt, vulnerability, fatigue, strange surroundings, unfamiliar faces, nakedness which she had never experienced before will heightens her anxiety in the labour room. The feeling that the possession she had carried for the past nine months is at danger may put her under further stress. Hence she fears not only for her life, but also for the baby. The abundance of oxytocin during the last stage of pregnancy helps to reduce her anxiety and keeps her feel calm and secure (Meyer, 2007).

Idealized picture of pregnancy, as a wonderful experience with less pain and great joy, creates a feeling of guilt if the women find the entire process as painful, if the pregnancy is from an unplanned or terminated relationship, this may further adds to the misery (Bobak & Jensen, 1995).

Having covered prenatal stress, it's major sources and adverse impacts, it is essential to have an understanding of stress in general and its underlying physiological and theoretical aspects before going into the details of its assessment.

Various Approaches in Stress Research

Three different ways in which the researchers had approached the concept 'stress' are: (a) as an environmental event, focusing on stressors or life events; (b) as a psychological process, assessing subjective stress appraisal and affective reactions; and (c) as a biological response, assessing the activation of the physiological systems involved in the stress response (Cohen, Kessler & Underwood, 1995; Kopp, Thege, Balog, Stauder, Salavecz, Rozsa, Purebl & Adam, 2010).

As suggested by Lazarus, stress is comprised of stressful events or conditions ("stressors"), perceptions or evaluations of these stressors ("appraisals"), and stress responses such as emotions (Lazarus & Folkman, 1984). It is the mental and physical responses and adaptation by our body to the real or perceived changes and challenges in our life. This multidimensional approach to understand the concept stress has got a more attention and is the most widely used approach by the researchers on Prenatal Maternal Stress.

A stressor may be perceived as a threat or a challenge; and based on one's perception their response also varies. Appraising an event as a threat is followed by a series of negative emotions such as fear, anxiety and anger; at the same time appraising them as challenge will leads to positive emotions such as excitement and eagerness. Stress in any given situation can be understood as the result of a cognitive appraisal process resulting in an emotional, physiological and behavioural stress response (Gaab, Rohleder, Nater & Ehlert, 2005).

Hence stress is the responses of brain and body to any demanding situation which is perceived as a threat or a challenge. In its basic survival mechanism brain initiates stress response which involves a series of hormonal responses triggered by hypothalamus. The hypothalamus stimulate pituitary gland in the brain which in turn stimulate adrenal gland on top of each kidney to release stress hormones, epinephrine or adrenaline, which prepares our body for the fight or flight response. These hormones triggers the Autonomous Nervous system (ANS) to increases the heart rate, breathing, blood pressure and blood flow to the muscles.

The primary stress hormones such as cortisol, adrenaline (epinephrine), and noradrenalin (norepinephrine), are released to provide instant energy, other parts of the brain and body release endorphins, which relieve pain caused by the stressor. As the body adjusts to chronic unresolved stress, the adrenal glands continue to release cortisol, which remains in the bloodstream for a prolonged period and it slows down our metabolic responsiveness. Prolonged presence of cortisol in blood reduces immune-competence (Cohen, Kessler & Underwood, 1995). Since the foetal level of cortisol also reflects the maternal level, prolonged exposure to stress hormones will results in infections among new-born due to compromised immune system.

The biopsychosocial model, widely used in disciplines such as Medicine, Psychology and Sociology is used in the study to understand prenatal stress. The model views stress as an outcome to the interaction of biological (genetic, biochemical etc.), psychological (mood, personality, behaviour, etc.), and social factors (cultural, familial, socioeconomic, medical, etc.). The model was first proposed by George L. Engel, a Physician in 1977. The model has helped to deconstruct the narrowly defined views on clinical conditions as a reflection of mere biological factor to a wider context by including psychological and social components.

During pregnancy women undergoes various physiological as well as psychological transformation, which makes them more vulnerable to many adverse social conditions. To understand the concept of prenatal stress it is essential to have a comprehensive understanding of the various factors that triggers prenatal stress. Hence the model has been used in the study to explore the possible dimensions of prenatal stress.

Assessment of Prenatal maternal stress

Though there is a tremendous increase in research on assessment of prenatal maternal stress, such measures are not always accompanied by theoretical grounding or psychometric evidences, resulting in serious questions about the quality and direction of theses research.

Emotional response to stress during pregnancy which is alternatively labelled in the literature as pregnancy-specific distress, worry, anxiety or stress, is an important component of prenatal maternal stress (Fiona & Lobel, 2012). Researchers show a clear distinction between general stress and pregnancy specific stress (Meades & Ayers 2011). Pregnancy specific stress includes those concerns which are very specific to a pregnant woman, such as the physical symptoms, changes in appearance, changes in interpersonal relations, labour and delivery, parenting concerns, health of the foetus and fear of medical complications etc. (Dunkel Schetter, 2011; Stanton et al, 2002).

Although pregnancy-specific stress tends to co-occur with general or non-specific stress during pregnancy, a variety of studies indicate that pregnancy specific stress could be a more powerful predictor of birth outcomes. This is further emphasized when many studies had failed to identify any general or nonspecific stress as a reliable predictor of preterm birth or other adverse birth outcomes (Glynn, Schetter, Wadhwa & Sandman, 2004). Studies also state that there is 1.5 to 2% greater risk to preterm birth among women with high pregnancy-related anxiety (Orr, Reiter, Blazer & James, 2007).

Reviews by Ross and McLean (2006), says that prevalence of prenatal stress is 0.6 to 7.7% and generalised anxiety disorders is 8.5% during perinatal period; this is same as, or higher than among general population. Though there is an increasing recognition on the prevalence and impact of stress and depression during prenatal period, screening of prenatal stress is warranted largely due to the fact that the measures currently available are too general or too specific to the extent that it covers only some specific aspect of pregnancy rather than serving as a comprehensive scale. This requires researchers to administer a battery of instruments to assess pregnancy specific stressors as well as general stress and anxiety among pregnant women, which is often impractical and time consuming in a health care setting.

Clinical representation of prenatal stress is largely undermined by the use of general stress measure. Since the unique experiences during pregnancy that generates a wide range of concerns which cannot be assessed adequately using a general stress measure (Arizmendi & Affonso, 1987) without considering any of the physiological, psychological and socioeconomic concerns of the pregnant women, such scales may deflate the scores and leaves the researcher with no further scope for interpretation.

Some of the widely used scales to assess prenatal stress are High Risk Pregnancy Stress Scale (HRPSS), Oxford Worries About Labour Scale (OWALS),

Prenatal Psychosocial Profile (PPP), Pregnancy Distress Scale etc. But these tools are designed to assess specific aspects of prenatal stress and were failed to serve as a comprehensive measure to assess prenatal stress. For example: Tilburg's 10 item Pregnancy Distress Scale (covers physical concerns of pregnancy, fear of delivery, intimate partner relation and economic factor to a great extent but failed to capture the emotional aspect, mood swings, intrapersonal relations with those other than spouse and experience of pregnancy from a more personal level. In High Risk Pregnancy Stress scale (HRPSS), since the items are focusing on high risk pregnancy, the scale is not suitable to assess prenatal stress among normal population (of low risk pregnancies of different parity and trimester). The OWALS, consist of items specific to labour pain, pre-labour uncertainty, and interventions, hence it focuses specifically on labour and birth and lacks the properties of a comprehensive prenatal stress scale. A-Z stress scale, developed after an in-depth interview with Pakistani pregnant women (Kazi, Fatmi, Hatcher, Niaz & Aziz, 2009) is another measure which assess pregnancy specific stress, but it limits it's scope to South Asian context. More over the scale focuses on listing down the stressors rather than considering how it is perceived by pregnant women, which further restricts it's scope.

Factors related to fears around pregnancy and childbirth, health of baby, concerns about changing relations and health of mother are some of the dimensions covered in various pregnancy specific scale. Items which are common among all prenatal stress measures are those relating to concern about physical changes or body image whereas anxiety about hospitalization is captured only in Pregnancy Anxiety Scale (PAS).

Studies in line with Lazarus' multidimensional approach conceptualising stress as a combinations of stressful events or conditions ("stressors"), perceptions or evaluations of these stressors ("appraisals"), and stress responses such as emotions offers more consistent and compelling evidence for adverse birth outcomes (Lobel et al., 1990).But such multidimensional approach is hardly used in research or in practice due to the absence of a comprehensive tool and the inability to use multiple test batteries or assessment techniques during the limited time available during consultation.

Hence having a comprehensive tool helps to provide better health care services, this facilitates an early diagnosis of risks involved and timely intervention. This prevents a large number of adverse birth outcomes as well as postnatal depression among women. Hence the challenge is to gear the research towards a measurement that captures the experience of the pregnant women comprehensively (Chandra & Ranjan, 2007).

Considering these limitations in the previous measures, the present study focuses on developing a multidimensional scale to assess prenatal maternal stress comprehensively. The first phase of the study focuses on exploring the components of prenatal stress further, through in depth interviews with pregnant women and thorough review of existing scales and literature in the area of prenatal stress for developing items for a comprehensive scale. Second phase focuses on validating the scale by assessing content validity and pilot testing and field testing the scale among pregnant women. The study also tries to explore the factorial composition of the scale through a factor analysis.

Literature Review

LITERATURE REVIEW

Pregnancy is a huge transition in women's life, involving complex mix of positive and negative emotions. Though the couple get almost nine months to adjust to the changes and prepare themselves to their new roles and responsibilities in parenthood, the pregnant women in particular have a difficult time indeed, since they are prone to wide variety of stressors ranging from pregnancy-specific issues such as, physical symptoms, issues associated with weight gain, low self-esteem, fear due to the risk associated with other medical co-morbidities, parenting concerns, emotional imbalances and mood swings due to hormonal changes, bodily changes, anxiety about labour and delivery and concerns about baby's health, appearance and other social factors such as lack of support from family, economic burden and relationship strains (Kornelsen, Stoll & Grzybowski, 2011; Yali & Lobel, 1999; Affonso & Mayberry, 1990) to more generic daily hassle (Woods, Melville, Guo, Fan & Gavin, 2010).

Prenatal Stress

Studies on prenatal stress covers a wide variety of stressors ranging from acute to chronic with altered child outcome. Studies on acute stressors include incidents or accidents such as exposure to 9/11 incident (Yehuda, Engel, Sarah, Brand, Seckl, Marcus & Berkowitz 2005), Chernobyl disaster (Huizink, Dick, Sihvola, Pulkkinen, Rose & Kaprio, 2007), Canadian ice storm (Laplante , Brunet, Schmitz, Ciampi & King, 2008) etc. or chronic stressors such as daily hassles or pregnancy specific anxiety (Huizink, Robles de Medina, Mulder, Visser, & Buitelaar, 2003).

Though there exists multiple studies that explore potential stressors which many women undergo during their pregnancy; it is difficult to give a comprehensive definition to prenatal stress, mainly due to the fact that stressors during pregnancy are highly nonspecific and is associated with women's idiosyncratic perception of these events as negative. Due to these individual variations same events or stressor might be perceived differently by different women and differently by the same at different situations.

Hence, Prenatal Maternal Stress (PNMS) is defined as 'any stressors which is perceived by pregnant women as emotionally or physically taxing or exceeding her resources or endangering her wellbeing'. This is in line with Lazarus and Folkman's (1984) definition of stress, which says: "a particular relationship between a person and the environment that is appraised by the person as taxing or exceeding his or her resources or endangering his or her wellbeing". Keeping this broader definition, Lobel (1994) had employed a multi-dimensional approach in his studies on PNMS and had found stressful prenatal life events predict lower birth weight (LBW; less than 2500 g) and younger gestational age at birth or preterm birth (at less than 37 weeks gestation) and maternal state anxiety predicts labor and delivery complications. Further research which employed a multidimensional approach to measure stressors and appraisal of stress responses (Lobel, 1994) predicts more convincing and compelling evidences on the risks of PNMS on adverse birth outcomes.

Both prospective and retrospective studies on the risks of prenatal maternal stress using both animal and human models states that: stress leads to undesired birth outcomes. Most of such prospective studies were carried out on animals by inducing stress or by injecting stress hormones in a laboratory setting, or by exposing them to extreme stressful conditions (Del Cerro, Pérez-Laso, Ortega, Martín, Gómez, Pérez-Izquierdo, & Segovia, 2010). Though there is a limitation for such studies on human model, there is substantial evidence which states: anxiety, depression, and stress during pregnancy are high risk for mothers as well as for the foetus, which mostly studied this construct retrospectively. More specifically these studies says anxiety during pregnancy is associated with shorter gestation, preterm birth, low birth weight (Copper et al., 1996; Dole, Savitz, Siega-Riz, Mc Mahon, & Buekens, 2003; Hedegaard, Henriksen, Secher, Hatch, & Sabroe, 1996) and adverse implications on foetus especially on neural development. Some studies also reports that exposure to extreme stressful events may leads to increased risk for autism disorder and other disorders such as schizophrenia and depression (Kinney, Miller, Crowley, Huang & Gerber, 2008) in later childhood, adolescence or in adulthood.

Programming effect of stress on foetus is well explored using foetal programming hypothesis. Prenatal stress leaves a programming effect on the foetus; that may affect the growth and development of the foetus and may impart an indelible impression on adult organ function, including the functioning of the brain and the nervous system. This hypothesis was strengthened by later studies which states; if the mother is prenatally stressed foetal level of cortisol will matches with that of the maternal level and prolonged exposure to these stress hormones may have an indelible impression on foetal brain and nervous system (Talge et al., 2007; Weissman, Warner, Wickramaratne, Moreau & Olfson 1997).

Due to the increasing recognition of harmful impacts of prenatal stress on fetal development this area has got wide attention of researchers and practitioners, and has triggered more prospective and retrospective studies using human model for more accurate results.

Theoretical Frame work

Despite a conclusive relationship between maternal psychosocial stressors and adverse pregnancy outcomes and foetal development, studies on PNMS has failed to create the right sense of seriousness about the concern among the health care professionals, this is mainly due to various factors: the foremost among these are the use of a deficient model to define PNMS use in various studies. This is not surprising since the construct, stress itself is relatively difficult to operationalize and most of the stress research were often hampered by methodological issues.

Use of conceptually vague and unconfirmed indicators of PNMS often leads to inconclusive results. Vague conceptualisation of PNMS considering only few stressors during this period rather than considering perceived stress, underestimated prenatal maternal distress in various studies. Hence the focus should have to be on exploring the vulnerabilities of pregnant women and assessing them based on how they perceive it. Following this approach some of the early studies focused on a vulnerability stress model assuming pregnancy itself presents unique psychological and social challenges.

Vulnerability-stress model. A large number of emotional disorders such as obsessive compulsive disorder, anxiety, depression etc. triggers with the onset of pregnancy.

In a study among 167 medically high risk pregnant women, Yali and Lobel (1999) had found experience of high levels of distress about preterm delivery, having an unhealthy baby, physical symptoms, labor and delivery and weight gain. The study further identified socio-demographic variables, including age, income, education, and parity have significant association with ways of coping adopted by these women. This means a better socioeconomic status and familiarity or knowledge about various stages and issues in pregnancy will help to adopt good coping strategies, where as a poor socioeconomic status is a potential source of stress.

This clearly demonstrates that there is a vulnerability-stress conceptualization during pregnancy (Brown & Harris, 1978). Studies indicates that pregnant women are vulnerable to stress and depression due to the risks associated with environmental factors such as unmet need for emotional support (Borders, Grobman, Amsden, Holl & Stewart, 2007) and socio-economic disadvantages (DiPietro, Novak, Costigan, Atella & Reusing, 2006).

Theory of cognitive appraisal. The Cognitive stress model or 'the theory of cognitive appraisal' was proposed by Lazarus and Folkman (1984). According to them stress is a two way process involving stressors from the environment and the subjective response of an individual, which explain the mental process influenced by the stressors. Appraisals refer to an evaluative framework which is utilized by an individual to make sense of events. It is the direct, immediate, and intuitive evaluations made on the environment in reference to personal well-being.

Though both vulnerability stress model and theory of cognitive appraisal conceptualises PNMS differently, it is required to follow a multidimensional approach which agrees pregnant woman are vulnerable to various stressors and perception of these stressors as real threat depends on their cognitive appraisal.

Hence the present study merges the vulnerability stress model and theory of cognitive appraisal to understand the events (stressors) as well as how it is being perceived by women during their pregnancy. The vulnerability stress model assumes that while being pregnant, women are more vulnerable to stress and depression and the cognitive stress model brings in the component of appraisal of events as stressors. Hence rather than listing down stressors or by looking generally on the perceived stress, the study focuses on developing a measure that is capable in assessing the perception of events during pregnancy as a real threat or stressor.

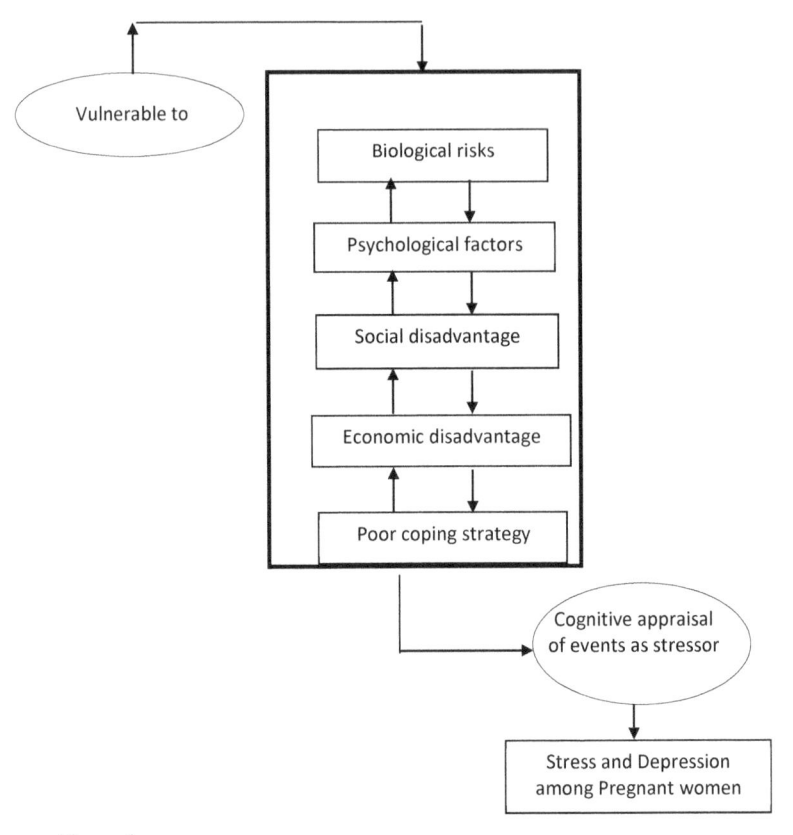

Figure 1
Diagram showing theoretical consolidation of prenatal stress

Stress and Depression during Pregnancy

Although exact figures of prevalence of prenatal stress is uncertain, published results shows it ranges from 5% to 25 % among new mothers in the postpartum period. It is 3.1% to 4.9% for major depression alone at different times during pregnancy and during post partum year, it is 1.0% to 5.9%. The combined estimates of major and minor depression at different times during pregnancy ranges from 8.5% to 11.0%, it is 6.6% to 12.9% at different time during postpartum. Studies reports that 18% of the pregnant women suffers from depression during pregnancy where as 13% experience major depression (Gavin, Gaynes, Lohr, Meltzer, Gartlehner & Swinson, 2005).

Studies also show that prenatal stress varies across pregnancy; 7% of women in their first trimester, 13% in the second trimester and 12% in third trimester (Gavin et al., 2005; Marcus, Flynn, Blow, & Barry, 2003) suffer stress and depression during their pregnancy.

Early studies on prenatal stress were mainly focused on relationship between maternal mental health, pregnancy outcome and infant growth. Various tools were used to assess prenatal stress ranging from measures on pregnancy specific stressors which measures stressful life events to measure on perception of these events or daily hassles. In a study conducted by Franck and colleagues among 114 pregnant never depressed women with a mean age of 29.5 years from a community health centre and a private hospital in Belgium, the researchers assessed the participants on their day to day fluctuations in mood and its possible risk for depression. The women were assessed during the second or third trimester of their pregnancy (time frame 1) and 12 weeks after their delivery (time frame 2). Day to day self-esteem and mood state were assessed during both the time frames. The results indicate that participants reported lower self-esteem mostly on those days on which they experienced more depressed mood. The study found significant inverse correlations between prenatal depressive symptomatology and level of self-esteem. The study also found a positive correlation between self-esteem instability and postnatal depression. Hence the study states that day to day levels of mood has an adverse impact on self-esteem and further on depressive symptoms during pregnancy. The study supports vulnerability stress model as well as the cognitive theory of depression that suggests unstable self-esteem could be a diathesis for depressive symptoms on individuals confronted with different life stressors (Clark, 1998).

Another study conducted on high risk sample to identify the role of optimistic dispositions on PNMS had identified an inverse association with PNMS and birth outcome (Lobel, De Vincent, Kaminer & Meyer, 2000). The study further says that optimists are more likely to exercise, and exercise is associated with lower risk of preterm delivery. Hence the study supports the argument that emotional response to pregnancy should be considered as a component while measuring PNMS rather than simply listing down the stressors since emotional response helps to understand her perception of stress as a real threat, which compromises her wellbeing.

A growing body of research demonstrates elevated anxiety during pregnancy predicts negative mental health outcomes for women (Huizink et al., 2004) and is also linked to negative birth and child outcomes (Lobel, 1994). A more focused research in this field had identified that Pregnancy-related anxiety is a unique construct and is distinct from general anxiety. This leads to more research with construct specific tools rather than a general anxiety scale to measure prenatal anxiety (Van den Bergh, 1990). This distinction bolstered with the careful analyses in the studies by Dunkel-Schetter and others (Dunkel-Schetter, 2009), who have shown that a specific type of anxiety known as "pregnancy anxiety" more robustly predicts negative outcomes such as pre-term birth than general anxiety and depression.

Though earlier studies were focused on limited aspects of prenatal stress, later studies tried to explore the construct in detail. Some of the major themes of pregnancy specific stressors covered in most of these studies are: fear of pain and delivery, physical changes during pregnancy, sex preferences and female infanticide or foeticide and other acute stressors like death of a family member or any catastrophes or other natural disasters of severe loss and social stigmas.

Some of the major concerns or focus areas of early studies on prenatal stress are intimate partner violence and compulsion for sex selective abortion. Atrocities against women in the familial and the societal setup were also identified as potential source for stress and depression.

Strains in intimate partner relation. While considering factors which leads to stress, studies shows that intimate partner violence (IPV) leads to poor satisfaction in marital relations. IPV is experienced by women in all age group despite of their economic status, race, religion, ethnicity or educational background and is most prevalent among women in reproductive age and this contributes to gynaecologic disorders, pregnancy complications, physical injury and psychological abuse (Brown, 2009).

Despite being a developed country, more than one in three women in United States experience rape, physical violence, or stalking by their intimate partner (Black, Basile, Breiding, Smith, Walters, Merrick, Chen & Stevens, 2010). But the victim hardly discloses their personal experience due to the fear of breakup. This will negatively affects the wellbeing and many studies associate risks such as infections due to compromised immune response, anaemia, tobacco use and other health compromising behaviours during pregnancy which leads to poor pregnancy such as: stillbirth, pelvic fracture, placental abruption, foetal injury, preterm delivery, and low birth weight (Brown, 2009).

Incidence of domestic violence against women in various countries is around 25% to 30%. Such violence also prevails during pregnancy and is found as a common and significant source of prenatal stress and postnatal depression among women. During pregnancy, studies show that this might reduce to 5%. In 90% of such cases, intimate partner is the main perpetrator (Bacchus, Mezey & Bewley, 2004).

In a retrospective study conducted among 9938 women who were 15 to 49 years, living with a child lesser than 18 years old in the rural and urban India shows a prevalence of moderate to severe level of spousal physical violence up to 13% during pregnancy (Peedicayil, Sadowisky, Jayaseelan, Shankar, Jain, Suresh & Bangdiwala, 2004). These include violent behaviours such as slap, hit, kick, beat, use of weapon and other harms. Eighteen percent of these women experienced at least one of these abuses and about 3% experienced all six.

Another study conducted in 2006 by Deepthi Varma and colleagues among 203 pregnant women in an antenatal clinic in Bangalore had assessed the prevalence of IPV during pregnancy and its relationship with mental health outcomes, including depression and post-traumatic stress disorder as well as depressive, somatic symptoms and life satisfaction. In the study 14% of the women experienced physical violence and 15% were reported psychological abuse by their partner. One half of these women reported ongoing abuse during pregnancy and life satisfaction was poorer among those with any form of such violence (Varma, Prabha, Chandra, Thomas & Carey, 2007). The level of education and employment of the woman has no effect on incidence of abuse. The prevalence of violence is more on socially unsupported women or when the male partner is less educated or he is in the habit of taking alcohol, opium or tobacco (Khosla, Dua, Devi & Sud, 2005).

Poor social support/ interpersonal relation. Social support is an important component during prenatal as well as postpartum period. Social support will helps women to adapt to new roles and to be more responsive to the baby and it facilitate their intimate relationship (Baker & Taylor, 1997). Lack of social support during the postpartum period may leads to depression among women and would negatively affect the health of the baby (Hung, 2007).

Few studies which attempts to view depression form an evolutionary perspective (Lilienfeld & Marino, 1999), had suggested it as an adaptive response stating it as a pathological condition which is mainly due to a mismatch between what was adaptive in an earlier environment and the world in which we live. This is mainly due to the fact that, our ancestors lived in groups and which may be the size of a community which had created a well-bonded social group. Since our brain has adapted to this, in order to promote fitness within the environment, it is common that in our modern urban society we feel lack of social support, and socially isolated (Gluckman, Hanson & Spencer, 2005). Hence social gatherings and ceremonies as a part of custom and tradition will help to improve women's perception of positive social support and has to be followed (Henshaw, 2003). Studies also show that social rituals during pregnancy as well as after delivery in the Asian culture helped to reduces postpartum depression among Asian women (Stern & Krukman, 1983).

Infanticide or foeticide. Foeticide or termination of pregnancy could be voluntarily either due to medical issues or preferences or less preferences for a child (boy or girl). Foeticide, especially due to compulsion from the family or spouse for medical concerns or for preferences for a male or a female child is extremely stressful for the mother after carrying her baby with her for some time. Female foeticide is more prevalent in south Asia, since the society has an intrinsic preference or inclination for male child due to cultural reasons. This leads to compulsion on women either from her family or from her partner for sex determination and selective abortion. This is considered as extremely painful and emotionally taxing for a mother and a potential source for prenatal stress which could have a negative implication on the growth and development of the foetus. Studies show that gender of the infant is a potential source of stress for pregnant women and a major determinant of postnatal depression (Patel, Rodrigues & De Souza, 2002). Such worries and concern will heighten if her first child is a girl.

In a study conducted among 270 mothers recruited at third trimester of pregnancy in a district hospital in Goa, depressive disorder was identified among 23% of mothers and 78% of these women had clinically substantial psychological morbidity during the antenatal period. The study then reviewed the babies of these

250 mothers, at birth on their weight and had found maternal psychological morbidity as an independent predictor low birth weight. The study identified economic deprivation and poor marital relationships were major risk factors for depression. The study concludes that psychological morbidity adversely affects foetal growth and development (Patel and Prince, 2006).

Incidence of pregnancy loss. Pregnancy loss, regardless of the type and timing, cause serious emotional strain and psychological stress among women, which may leads to depression and may follows in to subsequent pregnancies, especially those pregnancies immediately following the loss. Researches show that, such pregnancies may be complicated by heightened anxiety, than for those women who are pregnant for the first time or women who had a previous normal pregnancy (Armstrong, 2002).

A longitudinal study by Blackmore and colleagues (2011), aimed to assess the persistence of affective symptoms associated with previous loss conducted on 13133 mothers with conditions of prenatal loss have found, symptoms of depression and the anxiety associated with the event may persists as long as three years, even after a successful live birth (Blackmore, Côté-Arsenault, Wan Tang, Glover, Evans, Golding & O'Connor, 2011). The study concludes that these women were more likely to be diagnosed with depression (Giannandrea, Cerulli, Anson & Chaudron, 2013) hence requires a proper assessment and assistance.

Prenatal stress and health compromising behaviour. An indirect consequence of prenatal maternal stress is the adoption of certain health compromising behaviours. While being pregnant, if the women lacks a healthy coping strategy such as good interpersonal relationship or a happy family life, she may engages in various health compromising behaviours (Dennis, Ross, & Grigoriadis, 2007) such as smoking, use of drugs or alcohol or may even engage in poor diet (Ng & Jeffery, 2003) which are detrimental to health and may often leads to poor birth outcomes like low birth weight, preterm delivery and poor pregnancy outcome (Woods et al., 2010). Many researches supports the relation between maternal stress with poor nutrition, inadequate physical activity, cigarette smoking, and alcohol and other substance use *(Ahluwalia, Merritt, Beck, & Rogers, 2001; England, Kendrick, Gargiullo, Zahniser & Hannon, 2001; McDonald, Armstrong, & Sloan, 1995).*

Consumption of Alcohol during pregnancy is highly dangerous since it could cross the placenta and the foetal blood blain barrier and which could leads to FAS (Foetal Alcohol Syndrome). Conditions such as abnormal appearance, short height, low body weight, small head size, poor motor coordination, low intelligence, behaviour problems, and problems with hearing or vision are also associated with this (Chudley, 2005).

Though there exists multiple factors which contributes to prenatal maternal stress, studies had made a distinction between emotional responses to stressors during pregnancy, alternately labelled as prenatal maternal stress consisting of pregnancy-specific distress, worry or anxiety and more general stressors consisting of life events or global stressors (Huizink et al., 2003; Lobel et al., 2000).Though they may co-occur during pregnancy, studies failed to identify any general or non-specific stress as a reliable predictors of preterm birth (Dunkel-Schetter, 2011).

Further studies on prenatal maternal stress associate greater physiological arousal with pregnancy specific stressors than with general stress (DiPietro, Hawkins & Hilton, 2002). Some studies in this line associate higher foetal heart rate variability and foetal movements with higher scores on pregnancy-specific hassles but not with non-pregnancy-specific stress. Convergent validity of pregnancy specific stress measures also suggests that pregnancy-specific stress is related to, but distinct from, global stress.

Most of the pregnancy specific stress measures are built on concerns of pregnant women: such as, changes in their appearance, changes in interpersonal relations, physical symptoms during pregnancy, labour and delivery, parenting, health of the foetus and fear of medical complications. Studies that disregard these may underestimate the level and extent of stress that a woman may experience during pregnancy.

Studies on prenatal maternal stress focus more on pregnancy specific stressors, since the use of a multidimensional approach which assess stressful stimuli, appraisals, and responses is often impractical and time consuming in a health care setting due to absence of a comprehensive scale. Review of currently available pregnancy specific stress measures (Alderdice, Lynn & Lobel, 2012) has also found that measures are not always been accompanied by any theoretical ground or psychometric evidences thus compromising the quality and effectiveness of its use in further research and in clinical settings. Above all, most of these pregnancy specific stress measures failed to be a multidimensional tool for screening, since they focuses only on one or two aspects of pregnancy leaving behind a large number of experiences and concerns during pregnancy.

Pregnancy Specific Stress measure

The most commonly used pregnancy specific stress measures with their dimensions are discussed here.

A conclusive relationship between prenatal stress and birth outcome has triggered more interest among researchers for more prospective and retrospective studies on prenatal stress. As a result, evolved a number of pregnancy specific stress measures. Though there is an increase in prenatal maternal stress research, studies are not always accompanied by theoretical grounding or psychometric evidences, resulting in serious questions about the quality and direction of research on pregnancy-specific stress measures. Based on the published data on reliability and validity, this section consolidates current knowledge on pregnancy specific stress measures.

Studies used a wide range of approaches to operationalize the construct, PNMS and one of the early approaches is to measure stressor that is general or nonspecific to pregnancy. Though such an approach has methodological short comings general stress measures such as State-Trait Anxiety Inventory (STAI) and the Manifest Anxiety Scale (MAS) were used widely in prenatal stress research (Bayrampour, Ali, McNeil, Benzies, Tough & MacQueen, 2016). Due to the lack of subject matter specification both the reliability of measures and the concomitant validity of findings linking anxiety to pregnancy outcomes is uncertain in such studies.

Later research in this area identified pregnancy specific stress measures built on the concerns of pregnant women yields more reliable results. In the reviews of Dunkel- Schetter (Dunkel-Schetter, 2011) on prenatal maternal stress, they found it difficult to identify any forms of general, non-specific prenatal stress that are reliable predictors of preterm birth. Studies by Di Pietro also associate foetal heart rate variability in late pregnancy and foetal movement in pregnancy with higher scores on pregnancy-specific hassles but not with non-pregnancy-specific stress (Di Pietro et al., 2006). Hence many researchers warn against the use of a general stress scale in prenatal maternal stress research, though such practice is most prevalent.

Since 1970's researchers had started to use pregnancy specific stress measures along with general stress scale. The growing conformity of pregnancy specific stress with outcome has triggered more and more researches to identify life events which are considered as stressors during pregnancy. A number of such prospective and retrospective studies were conducted across the world, with most of such research confines to US and UK. These studies had found that prenatal maternal stress is having a predictive validity on preterm birth (at less than 37 weeks gestation) and low birth weight (LBW; less than 2500 g), which are major causes of morbidity and mortality among newborns (Dunkel Schetter, 2011). In addition, association of prenatal maternal stress has been found with increased caesarean delivery and incidents of complications during labor and delivery (Dunkel Schetter, 2011).

As mentioned earlier these studies had employed various approaches to conceptualize and operationally define the construct PNMS based on its measures, which can be grouped into three heads: measures which focuses on pregnancy specific events or hassles (can be viewed as stressor measures), measures which focuses on whether the woman is anxious, concerned, or stressed rather than explicitly mentioning the stressors (appears to be an emotional response measure that is pregnancy-specific) and finally the multidimensional approach, which not only focuses on conditions or events that creates concerns or distress for pregnant women, but also the extent to which they perceive it as real stressor. In this third approach: the occurrence of stress, it's appraisal at personal level, and response to this are collapsed into items that ask women how worried or upset they are. These items cover various aspects such as physical symptoms during pregnancy, concerns of having an unhealthy baby, concerns about their labour and delivery, changes in roles and relationships etc.

Such a multidimensional approach to prenatal maternal stress was introduced by Lobel, (1994) by conceptualising stress as a combination of stressful events or conditions ("stressors"), perception or evaluations of these stressors ("appraisals"), and stress responses such as emotions, in line with the definition of stress given by Lazarus.

This is considered as the best approach to study PNMS and offers a stronger theoretical and empirical foundation for research rather than focusing on events or stressors alone. Various measures were developed over years which either focuses on pregnancy specific event or emotional response to these events or using a multidimensional approach. The number of items in each of these measures varies from 2 to 55. While majority of these scales uses Likert type response. Two scales PAS (Pregnancy Anxiety Scale) and PSEI (Prenatal Social Environment Inventory) use a dichotomous response. These measures were developed in different countries with a majority of being developed in the USA. Few among these measures, having considerable psychometric properties are discussed in detail.

Pregnancy Anxiety Scale (PAS). The Pregnancy anxiety scale, a 25 item true or false scale was developed by Burstein in 1974. The scale was validated in a sample of 61 normal pregnant women in Montreal. The scale is hardly followed up or used in later research for almost two decades due to the limited data on reliability and validity (Alderdice et al., 2012). The factor structure of the scale was also not explored by the author.

Later on, the scale was adapted by Levin in 1991, who reduced the PAS to a 10 item scale based on items loading on first order factors in a Confirmatory Factor Analysis. The three major factors identified in his study are: anxiety about being pregnant, anxiety about child birth and anxiety about hospitalization. The study was conducted in a hospital in Texas, retrospectively among postpartum Anglo, Hispanic and Black single mothers (N=266) soon after their delivery. Hence the study suffers from memory-linked under-recall (Jenkins, Hurst, and Rose 1979). Evidences suggests that retrospective recall can be problematic since retrospective accounts of negative and positive affect are prone to bias by exaggeration.

However the three factor model explored by Levin in his study indicate that a factor structure conceptually based on pregnancy experiences may be valid and meaningful (Levin, 1991). These findings had encouraged to develop more dimensionally comprehensive measures with items specific to situations. The revised measure is better suited for retrospective administration to assess anxiety about pregnancy. Since the study was conducted retrospectively using single African American mothers more studies needs to be done on a large and more diverse sample.

One of the other major drawback of the scale is that it uses a dichotomous (true/false) response which limits its ability to assess the intensity of anxiety experienced by the women during this period. Due to this limitation of dichotomous items a proxy measure for internal reliability (KR 20) was reported instead of Cronbach's alpha coefficient.

Though the tool has good psychometric properties, PAS items were originally written to tap anxieties about very specific and limited aspects related to pregnancy and childbirth, hence the scale is not expected to factor ideally in theoretical term. This had questioned the comprehensibility and multidimensionality of the scale, since emotional response or anxiety is just one aspect among its components.

Pregnancy Related Anxiety Questionnaire. PRAQ was developed by Van den Bergh in 1990. This is a lengthy measure with 55 items. A short version of this scale having 34 items is also available (Van Bussel, Spitz, & Demyttenaere., 2009). A longitudinal study was conducted on a convenience sample of 403 Belgium; ≥18 years old low-risk pregnant women, among them majority were married/ co-habiting, well educated, and belongs to 8–36 weeks of gestation. High rate of attrition is a major issue identified in the study. Reliability of the scale is 0.95, the scale has good internal consistency, validity scores for the 55 item original version is not available. A revised, shorter version of the scale consisting of 34 items having 5 point response was developed later (Huizink, Delforterie, Scheinin, Tolvanen, Karlsson, 2015) and used in various studies with samples ranging from 112-230, low risk pregnant women among 15–38 weeks of gestation. EFA of this scale identified factors such as: Fear of giving birth, Fear of bearing a physically or mentally handicapped child, fear of changes and disillusion in partner relationship, fear of changes, concern about one's mental well-being and the mother-child relationship. In the Confirmatory Factor Analysis (Huizink et al., 2004) factors identified are: fear of giving birth, fear of bearing a physically or mentally handicapped child and concerns about one's own appearance during pregnancy.

Reliability of the shorter version was calculated using Cronbach Alpha, the scale has good reliability 0.73– 0.88 and convergent validity on Perceived Stress Scale ($r = 0.20$, $p < 0.05$) and Daily Hassles scale ($r = 0.19$, $p < 0.05$) (Huizink et al., 2004) are also found significant.

Pregnancy outcome questionnaire. Pregnancy Outcome Questionnaire is a context specific scale that assesses anxiety during pregnancies subsequent to a perinatal loss. The scale was developed by Theut in 1988. The study considered 403 well educated, low risk pregnant women having age ≥18 years, majority married/ cohabiting and belongs to 8–36 weeks gestation. Later on three studies conducted in US and UK had used this scale but in a limited sample of 31-206 pregnant women with previous perinatal loss, in their second & third trimester of pregnancy (Armstrong, 2004).

The items such as "I feel confident that my pregnancy will proceed without any special problems" and "I worry about whether I will be able to bring this pregnancy to term" are framed in the context of previous perinatal loss. However, a few items are similar to other pregnancy-specific measures, for example, "I feel worried about the health of my new baby"; but a large span of prenatal worries was not adequately covered in the scale, failing this to be a comprehensive measure.

No predictive validity was established in any of these studies and no factorisation done for this 15 item four point Likert scale. Psychometric data is limited to internal consistency (0.80– 0.89) and convergent validity. Psychometric data on convergent validity shows significant correlation of prenatal stress on the scale with STAI – trait ($r = 0.47$–0.59, $p < 0.01$), Impact of Event Scale ($r = 0.57$, $p < 0.001$); Centre for Epidemiological Studies-Depression, CES-D ($r = 0.53$, $p = 0.001$) and Prenatal attachment ($r = -0.33$, $p = 0.05$). While observing the results, it is noted that though the correlation is significant the scale has a weak or moderate correlation with most of the scale, used to assess its validity, this clearly indicates the scale could capture only one dimension of prenatal stress i.e. stress following a prenatal loss.

The scale is best suited as a complimentary measure to be administered along with a general stress scale, or a comprehensive measure on prenatal maternal stress and its use is limited to evaluate anxiety in pregnancies subsequent to perinatal loss.

Pregnancy stress rating scale. PSRS was developed by Chen in 1989 with a small sample of 65 healthy, low-risk pregnant women from Taiwan, majority were married, who are in their 1st to 3rd trimester of pregnancy (Chen et al., 1989). Twenty eight items in the scale were distributed under three factors, where factor one captures: "stress from seeking safe passage for herself and her child through pregnancy, labor and delivery," containing 11 items; factor two: "stress from Identifying maternal role", containing 12 items; and factor three: "Stress from altering body structure and body function", containing 5 items. Factor loading of these items on respective factors ranges from 0.33 to 0.87.

The scale had recognized the most important and underlying component of pregnancy: i.e. the role change in motherhood along with other factors such as stress of pregnancy and childbirth (e.g. "afraid, baby will not be normal") and altered body (e.g. "worry about figure changes") which are similar to other prenatal stress scales. The factor "stress from identifying with maternal role" is composed of items such as: "difficulty in deciding the place for puerperium", "worry about future child rearing problems" which are not adequate to capture emotional conflicts associated with motherhood and role change during the prenatal stage. Other than factor analysis, reliability and validity of the scale were not reported. The instrument also fails to incorporate socio-economic variables such as: economic concerns and interpersonal relations that considerably alter stress experienced by pregnant women.

Pregnancy experience questionnaire (PEQ). PEQ, is a 42 item 3-point response scale, developed by Da Costa in 1998. Items were derived from scales on psychosocial stressors, maternal adjustment and attitudes. The author was able to bring in a wide range of stressors as against the previous measures, and it includes: stressors of somatic symptoms of pregnancy, fetus/infant and parenting concerns, attitudes towards sex of the baby and body image.

Three studies had used the scale to measure prenatal stress over the course of pregnancy: from 8 weeks of gestation to 4-5 weeks postpartum (Da Costa, Larouche, Drista & Brender, 2000) on low-risk naturally conceived women ranging from 19 to 40 years, in Canada. One of the interesting finding by the author is the variability on PEQ scores across trimesters suggesting a 'U' shaped pattern with the lowest scores in the second trimester. But one of the major concern was the sample size in these studies, which is very small ranging from 80-161. Further research needs to be done to confirm such critical window of prenatal stress and its impact on birth outcome using larger sample. Some of the early studies also tried to differentiate prenatal stress across the span of pregnancy in the same line, but the findings are contradictory, for example: longitudinal data on both versions of the PES (longer and shorter) shows, frequency and intensity of prenatal stress remain stable over pregnancy from the second trimester (Monk, Leight, Fang et al., 2008). Hence the results are not conclusive.

The scale has good reliability (0.87– 0.91). Convergent validity with Hassles scale and STAI-state ($r = 0.35$–0.65, $p < 0.001$) is also assessed. No predictive validity data were reported and the major drawback was the sample sizes were really small in all studies. Though the scale covers a wider area as compared to other scales, some of the major concerns like emotional concerns, economic factors, career related aspirations and the feeling of guilt are neglected.

Prenatal distress questionnaire. The 12 item Prenatal Distress Questionnaire (PDQ) was developed by Yali and Lobel in 1999. Later on, the test was used in four different studies (Lobel et al., 2000; Lynn, McElnay, 2010) with a sample ranging from 59 to 263, low- & high-risk pregnant women in the age group of 18 years or above who are in their 10 to 37 weeks of gestation. EFA of the scale suggested three factors such as "concerns about birth/baby,""concerns about weight/body image," and "concerns about emotions/ relations" (Yali & Lobel, 1999). All these studies were conducted in USA in a sample of diverse ethnicity, parity, marital status and socio economic status.

In a prospective, descriptive study conducted by Gennaro (2008) with a small sample of 59 black pregnant women, using Prenatal Distress Questionnaire and Perceived Stress Scale (a general stress scale) to measure the scale's validity along with corticotrophin-releasing hormone (a more reliable biological parameter), had failed to identify any strong correlation between the two stress measures as well as with corticotrophin-level. This has strengthened the doubts on the validity of self-report inventories to assess PNMS. The results say that stress at 28 weeks as measured by Prenatal Distress Questionnaire and Perceived Stress Scale was at its highest, but corticotrophin-level is higher at 32 weeks and then decreased towards the end. Though there is a discrepancy among measures the study supports the possibility of a critical window, but at the same time it is uncertain to associate a particular time frame as more vulnerable for fetus. The study strongly support the role of ethnic variations in the perception of prenatal stress and suggested further research, since perceived stress levels among Black women experiencing preterm labor around 28 weeks had differentiated Black women from women who delivered preterm infants. This says that there is a potential risk or vulnerability associated with being in a particular ethnic group beyond the fact that the women were prenatally stressed or not, hence the studies in future should have to moderate for the same.

Another interesting study using the scale was done by Lynn & Alderdice (2010), among a group of 263 healthy, low-risk pregnant women and the purpose of the research was to relate the level of stress with a number of maternal characteristics. The study was done in an urban maternity centre in Northern Ireland. The mean prenatal distress score of the sample was 15.1 ($SD = 7.4$; *range* 0-46). The regression model shows primiparous women have higher prenatal distress score as compared to women who had previous pregnancies with or without complications ($p < 0.01$).The study further says that lower age (16-20) and poor physical health are determinants of prenatal distress. The study suggests that an early identification of stress levels by an assessment tool or through specific associated factors identified within provides valuable data on maternal well-being. The study reminds ones again about the lack of availability of a comprehensive stress measure.

The scale has good internal consistency (0.80). Convergent validity was also assessed in various studies using Perceived Stress Scale (PSS) ($r = 0.37$–0.56, $p < 0.01$), STAI-state ($r = 0.55$, $p < 0.01$), Edinburgh Postnatal Depression Scale (EPDS) ($r = 0.33$–0.34, $p < 0.05$) and Life Experiences Survey (LES) ($r = 0.32$–0.37, $p < 0.05$). All the 12 item in the scale are related to pregnancy, but the items lack specificity and clarity. Though the scale is intended to assess prenatal stress, the scale in it's present form could capture only few specific stressors which are directly results from pregnancy, at the same time the whole range of aspects which are considered as stressors during pregnancy are neglected. This is very much evident from the weak or moderate correlation with other stress scales. Few of the items were found inappropriate or wrongly worded, for example: "The pregnancy has brought my partner and I closer together"; it's hard to say that the women may feel concerned or stressed if the pregnancy didn't brought the partners more closer, on the other hand she may feel concerned if her partner is uncaring or inattentive. Hence it is better to measure the satisfaction in intimate partner relation during the prenatal period; which is not at all considered in the scale. Hence few items failed to capture those dimensions which it really meant to. Another item, "Concern about this pregnancy" is too vague and broad. Considering the multidimensionality o the scale, it compromises the very purpose of it.

Pregnancy experience scale (PES). Fourty one item, Pregnancy Experience Scale was developed in 1999 using a very limited sample of 120 healthy low-risk pregnant women. The measure contains two sub scales: hassles and uplifts. An uplift scale is included since it is assumed that: measurement of only 'negative aspects' of pregnancy will overestimate distress and may fail to portray the degree to which women were psychologically elevated by their pregnancies (Dipietro, Christensen, Costigan, 2009). Thus by measuring uplifts and hassles the scale provides a more balanced assessment of pregnancy specific events. The PES uses a 4-point Likert scale on which, participants have to respond how much an item makes them feel "happy, positive, or uplifted" on the uplift scale and how much an item makes them feel "unhappy, negative, or upset" on the hassles scale.

Most of the items are specific to pregnancy and associated events. In the 41 item version, each item could be rated in both dimensions, i.e. both as uplift and a hassle. The scale is aimed to assess the daily minor challenges related to pregnancy and to acknowledge the positive emotions a woman feels during this time. The hassles subscale have 20 items and the EFA has identified 5 factors such as preparation for baby, change in lifestyle, relationships, pregnancy concerns and body image (Bayrampour, Ali, McNeil, Benzies, Tough, & MacQueen, 2016).Various studies over time had reported a reliability of 0.91– 0.95. Convergent validity with some other stress scales were reported in few studies: with CESD ($r = 0.33$– 0.48, $p < 0.01$); with STAI ($r = 0.34 - 0.39$, $p < 0.01$); with Daily Stress Inventory ($r = 0.25$–0.35, $p < 0.05$) and Affect Intensity Measure ($r = 0.24 - 0.44$, $p < 0.05$).

The length of the tool and it's applicability among some sections of population, particularly those from low literacy levels, is a major concern. Hence later researchers had developed an abbreviated version of the PES by drawing the most frequently endorsed items from the original PES. The PES-Brief consists of 10 items on each subscale (Dipietro, Christensen, Costigan, 2008). The revised scale considered a very limited sample: 94 healthy, low-risk pregnant women, from USA: majority non-

Hispanic White, married, nulliparous, well educated, 24 – 38 weeks of gestation. Reliability of the revised version is 0.830.45 – 0.77 and convergent validity was reported using: STAI ($r = 0.27$– $0.59, p < 0.05$); CESD ($r = 0.35$–$0.66, p < 0.05$).

Both the original and revised study devised a longitudinal, prospective design with convenient sample. There are evidences of selection bias, with high rate of attrition in the study (Monk et al., 2008). As against the widely held belief that stress varies throughout pregnancy, interestingly longitudinal data on both versions of the PES shows, frequency and intensity remain stable over pregnancy from the second trimester. But the study has no conclusive data on first semester.

If we consider the draw backs of this scale: no data available on predictive validity in any of the studies. The sample size considered by the scale is very limited and is just 189, hence the reliability and validity of the scale needs to be further investigated. One of the major limitation of the items are, rather than trying to capture the emotional experience of women during pregnancy the scale simply lists down the events associated with pregnancy. Some of the items are too vague such as "normal discomforts of pregnancy", "Spiritual feelings about being pregnant" and the scale also failed to be a comprehensive measure since it lacks many aspects such as intrapersonal or emotional variations during pregnancy, career related concerns and interpersonal relations except relations with intimate partner. Since the items are not strongly worded to capture the emotional aspects of pregnancy hence it appears like another stressor measure. For example: "Clothes/ shoes don't fit, "Your weight", "Getting enough sleep", "Baby showers for you", "Baby's sex" are almost like listing down the stressors rather than trying to capture the underlying emotional response.

The A – Z stress scale. This is one among the context specific scale developed for specific group: South Asian women. It was developed with Pakistani population keeping South Asia as the wider context.

Items were constructed based on interviews with 25 experts and 79 women in Pakistan (Kazi et al., 2009). The scale consist of 30 items covering a wide range of stressors including personal finance, intimate partner and culture specific items such as 'concerns about giving birth to a girl child'. It covers family-related concerns (with husband, children, in-laws and parents), socioeconomic concerns and pregnancy-related concerns. The maximum possible score on A–Z Stress Scale is 179. Based on the interview the scale has tried to include all the items which are perceived as stressors by pregnant women in South Asian context, in their past one month of pregnancy. Considering the importance of the intimate partner, seven items are directly related to intimate partner relations.

The scale was administered among 342 Pakistani pregnant women belonging to varied socio-economic group and gestational age. The study considered a convenient sample with the risk of selection bias. The author hadn't worked out the factor structure of the scale. The scale has good internal consistency (Cronbach's Alpha is 0.75 - 0.86) and test retest reliability (.86). The convergent validity of the scale was assessed using Centre for Epidemiologic Studies Depression Scale (CESD) ($r = 0.56$, $p < 0.001$).

Two dimensions of the scale were determined by the author using multidimensional scaling: socio-environmental hassles and chronic illnesses. The scale has rightly identified some of the culture specific items such as "concern about giving birth to a girl child". Items like "Concern about gaining supremacy among in-laws", "Concern about rented home" are too general. Items are largely concerned with the events associate with the normal life rather than events specific to pregnancy and experience of being a pregnant woman. There is a chance for this may unnecessarily inflate scores on stress or ignores scores on pregnancy specific concern; which is supposed to be the key concern. Chances for these are higher, since the dimensions are limited to socio-environmental hassles and chronic illnesses.

Table 1:

Table below shows the properties of various Pregnancy Specific Stress Measures

Measure	Item	Scale type	Dimension
A–Z Stress Scale	30	10 point scale	Socio-environmental hassles Chronic illnesses
Pregnancy Anxiety Scale	25	Dichotomous	No dimensions
Pregnancy Experience Scale (PES) – hassles subscale	20	4-point scale	Preparation for baby, Change in lifestyle, Relationships, Pregnancy concerns and Body image/self
Pregnancy Distress Questionnaire	12	5 point Scale	Concerns about birth/baby, Concerns about weight/body-image, Concerns about emotions/relations
Pregnancy Outcome Questionnaire (POQ)	15	4-point Scale	
Pregnancy stress rating Scale (PSRS)	30	4-point Scale	Labour and Delivery, Maternal Role and Body Changes
Pregnancy Experience Scale	41	4-point Likert Scale	Hassles and uplifts
Pregnancy Related Anxiety Questionnaire	34 (revised)	5-point Likert Scale	Fear of giving birth, Fear of bearing a physically or mentally handicapped child, fear of changes and disillusion in partner relationship, fear of changes, concern about one's mental well-being and the mother-child relationship
Pregnancy Experience Questionnaire	42	3-point Likert Scale	Items were derived from measures of psychosocial stressors, maternal adjustment and attitudes.

Note: Table showing the properties of various stress measures

Empirical studies examining the impact of pregnancy-specific stress on birth outcomes using multidimensional assessment scales and general stress scale will determine whether PNMS have a superior predictive validity. But as mentioned before most of these measures having multidimensional approach lacks the comprehensibility. As a result the researchers as well as practitioners need to use a battery of tests which is either cumbersome or time consuming. Though it could be practical in a research setting, it is hardly possible for practitioners due to time constrains.

From the review it is clear that, though the current level of achievement on prenatal stress measures is commendable, more research needs to be done to achieve the character of a comprehensive scale. This is required to improve the reliability and predictive validity of such measures over varied sample and across pregnancy. Since the aim of this study is to explore various stressors which a pregnant women is exposed to, and to identify the extent to which they perceive it as a real threat and their reaction to this, the study tries to capture the construct PNMS in the most comprehensive way as compared to the previous studies.

Since there is a growing evidence of prenatal maternal stress on pregnancy outcome, timely interventions to deal with pregnancy specific stress will prevent the risk to premature birth and other adverse impacts. Intervention that addresses a specific concern by creating awareness or by extending support to women in relation to concerns over pregnancy and childbirth may be more effective than global, untailored techniques in addressing their stress. To identify such specific concerns of pregnant women it is essential to have a comprehensive tool that could efficiently capture a wide range of concerns.

Summary

Extreme stressful circumstances during pregnancy often associated with work pressure, break-up of marriage, physical or emotional abuse, open infidelity or simply disinterested or uninvolved partners could have a negative impact on the behavior and biology of the offspring.

Despite cultural background, women during their pregnancy were exposed to varied physiological, psychological and social stressors. Various approaches were used in the previous studies to assess prenatal maternal stress, by using a pregnancy specific measure or a general stress measure or both. Since general stress measures are not as efficient as pregnancy specific stress measure in predicting the outcome; a number of latter studies in this area were focused on developing a pregnancy specific stress measures. But most of these tools failed to be a comprehensive measure which views pregnancy as an experience having multiple dimensions. Most of these scales also have limited psychometric properties and theoretical underpinning.

In the absence of a firm estimate of prenatal stress and an agreement on appropriate screening tool, it is difficult to provide proper care and support to the women who are in dire need. To address this and to ensure the wellbeing of the mother and the child to be borne, a proper assessment of prenatal stress, which employs a multidimensional approach, is very much essential.

Objectives

Though general stress and pregnancy specific stress measures are found to predict preterm birth, poorer neonatal behavioural outcomes (Talge et al., 2007) and social developmental outcomes (Wadhwa, 2005), there is also a suggestion that pregnancy specific stressors are more potent type of stressor as compared to general stressors as a better predictor of preterm birth (Lobel & Dunkel Schetter, 1990). This has created a need among researchers and practitioners for a more comprehensive and a robust tool that adequately measure prenatal maternal stress.

The objective of this study is to conduct a rigorous, theoretically driven, psychometrically robust research on prenatal stress to develop a comprehensive scale which equips the health care professionals and researchers with a measure that will meet the requirements for a multi cohort panel study. Accordingly, the scale should be applicable at any stage of pregnancy and among women belonging to different age, parity and socioeconomic background.

The major question the researcher faces while engaging in such a complex task is: "What should be the various dimensions of such a measure which assess PNMS comprehensively?" To answer this, it is required for the researcher to explore through the experience of pregnant women belonging to different parity and trimester. To realise this challenge and to develop a comprehensive measure, the first phase of this research entirely focuses on an exploratory study on prenatal stress and development of items, whereas the second phase focuses on assessing reliability and validity of items and exploring the factor structure of the scale.

Method

METHOD

Phase 1: Development of Items and Content Validity Assessment by Subject Matter Experts

This initial phase of the study involves determining content domain, development of item pool and establishing content validity of items. The framework of the scale was set to a wider domain covering women belonging to different parity and trimester. To develop an initial content domain of the construct, existing stress measures and published literature on PNMS were thoroughly reviewed. Directions and opinions were also sought from experts including gynaecologists, psychologists and nurses. A semi structured guideline was developed from this initial construct to conduct an in depth interview with pregnant women with the objective of gaining clear insight into to the concerns and worries of pregnant women belonging to different gravidity, parity and diverse economic background. These interviews were helped to compensate the gaps in the knowledge obtained from the existing scales and literature on PNMS.

Procedure. Women belonging to socioeconomically diverse population of different parity and trimester were considered during this phase. The participation was voluntary and they could withdraw from the study at any stage, without any penalty. Each interviewee had given a brief description about the objectives of the study.

Interviews were conducted in a private clinic. The interviewer had ensured the convenience of the interviewee for a free and fair response. Typically, each of the interviews begins with a brief introduction by the interviewer about the purpose of the interview followed by some background questions about the interviewee such as parity, stage of pregnancy, education, occupation etc.

Considering the objective of the study, interviews were largely unstructured. The interviewees were asked to share their experience and various "concerns", "difficulties" and "stressful events" they had experienced so far in their pregnancy. Since the interviews were conducted in a hospital setting, the interviewees were open to share their experience considering it as a part of health care system. Though few areas were not initially touched upon, especially topics such as intimate partner relations, economic concerns; they revealed more and more about the nature of their relation, approach of their partner to their pregnancy and how they perceive it, as and when the interview progress.

The interviewer tried to avoid leading the interview and not to interrupt in between the conversation to retain the flow of the conversation. Before winding up each interview the interviewee were asked: "Is there anything else that you would like to tell me?" Each interview lasted for 60 minutes and was ended with a closing statement by thanking the participants. Immediately after the interview the interviewer took time to fill the gaps in the notes and to emphasis any newly identified concerns and overall impression about the interview. The interviewer often used probes such as: "What did you mean when you said…?", "Could you give me an example on how it feels when it happened to you?", "Why do you think so?" or "How did you perceived it at that time?", to get more insight into their experience.

Considering the objectives of this qualitative phase, interviews were continued only unto a point of data saturation. Twenty five such interviews were conducted until the list of stressors seems redundant and terminated after since no new stressors were identified. This qualitative phase, the interviews of those who experienced the phenomenon, had helped to enrich and develop what has already been known about the construct from earlier reviews.

Based on the insights from reviews and interviews a list of various concerns of pregnant women was prepared such as intimate partner relations , social support, mood swings, weight gain and other emotional and physical concerns during pregnancy, economic concerns, poor planning and preparedness for pregnancy, fear of labour and delivery, concerns about baby's gender and physical appearance and career related compromises during pregnancy (Table 3).

The next step in the process is to construct a number of items which are capable to capture these concerns.

The designing stage is followed by a quantitative phase, which begins with assessment of content validity of the items using Content Validity Ratio (CVR) (Lawshe, 1975) by 23 SMEs. I-CVI and S-CVI was also used in this phase to assess the content validity of individual item and the entire scale.

Content validity analysis. Next step in the process is to assess content validity of the items by a panel of subject matter experts (SME).This is to determine the appropriateness of each of the item with respect to the given construct. Lawshe's (1975) content validity ratio (CVR), a widely practiced method for gauging agreement among SMEs was used in the study.

CVR procedure. To examine CVR, 23 SMEs, including gynaecologists, nurses and psychologist were identified. They were briefed about the purpose of the study and the method followed in construction of initial 40 items. These SMEs were asked to rate each item into one of the three categories: "essential," "useful, but not essential," or "not necessary," in a 3- point Likert scale based on how essential they think a particular item is to measure the underlying construct PNMS. These SMEs were also asked to express their suggestions and over all opinion about the items and the scale.

Under Lawshe's method, content validity is determined by CVR (Lawshe, 1975) which is expressed as:

$$CVR = \frac{(N_e - N/2)}{(N/2)}$$

Where:

N_e = the number of SMEs indicating an item as "essential",

N = the total number of SMEs

The CVR range from $^+1$ (perfect agreement) to $^-1$ (perfect disagreement); a positive value indicate that at least half of the SME have rated the item as "essential" and the item have some content validity. If CVR = 0, indicate that 50% of the SME had rated the item as "essential".

To avoid the element of chance, CVR of each of these items has to be compared with the critical value: CVR $_{critical}$ (Lawshe, 1975). Items having a CVR equal or greater than this critical value were retained where as those falling to achieve this were discarded. A lower CVR for an item signifies that, the item seemed unable to measure the desired concept by the SMEs. The critical value is determined from the table of critical values (Wilson, Pan & Schumsky, 2012) by considering number of items in the scale and SMEs who rated the scale. This critical value for the present study is 0.391.

S-CVI (Scale Content Validity Index) procedure. Content validity concerns the degree to which a scale has an appropriate sample of items to represent the construct of interest, a scale-level content validity, tells this explicitly. There are alternative ways to compute the S-CVI (Polit & Beck, 2006). The most widely used approach for the S-CVI is to compute the I-CVI for each item on the scale, and then average I-CVI across items. S-CVI is the agreement among the judges for the entire instrument and is calculated only for relevancy.

For the purpose of assessing the S-CVI, the same experts were asked to rate the relevance of each item on a 4-point scale. The 4 ordinal points were labelled as: 1 = not relevant; 2 = somewhat relevant; 3 = quite relevant; 4 = highly relevant (see Appendix). Then, for each item, the I-CVI is computed as the number of experts giving a rating of either 3 or 4, divided by the number of experts, that is, the proportion of agreement about the relevance of item among the SMEs. For example: an item rated as "quite" or "highly" relevant by 4 out of 5 judges would have an I-CVI of .80. Items with scores of over 0.75 were considered as appropriate.

Scale developers often use a criterion of .80 as a statistically acceptable limit for S-CVI (Polit & Beck, 2006). The procedure for calculating S-CVI is given below.

$$S\text{-}CVI = \frac{\text{Sum of I-CVI}}{N}$$

Where N is the total number of items.

This phase is followed by pilot testing and field testing of the newly developed measure in a sample 356 pregnant women. Cronbach's alpha is used to determine internal consistency reliability of the scale and exploratory factor analysis (EFA) was conducted to determine the underlying factor structure, which is followed by assessing a best fit model for the construct PNMS using Confirmatory Factor Analysis (CFA), these are explained in detail in the next chapter. Convergent and divergent validity of the newly developed measure was also assessed on 10 item Perceived Stress Scale (PSS) and WHO (Five) Well-being index (1998). The procedure is detailed in phase 2 of this chapter.

Phase 2: Standardization of the Scale

This quantitative phase focuses on pilot testing and field administration of the newly developed scale having 31 items for the purpose of assessing reliability and validity and exploring the underlying factor structure of the scale.

Sampling technique. All participants considered in the study are pregnant women in the age group of 20 to 35, having conceived naturally to ensure identical factor solution in terms of number of factors extracted and factor structure. Within this population of pregnant women, maximum diversity was ensured by don't limiting the pregnant women to a specific parity, trimester or other socioeconomic variables since limited heterogeneity have ramifications for the accuracy of factor analysis. To ensure this, the study was conducted in a cosmopolitan city, Delhi, the national capital of India. Being a capital city, Delhi has a diverse population from varied socioeconomic and cultural background.

To include pregnant women belonging to diverse background, the study had considered two popular hospitals, Tirath Ram Shah and St. Stephen's Hospital in Tiz hazari, Delhi; both are having a good inflow of patients from diverse background for antenatal check-ups. Both the hospitals have general OPD and private OPD, women from upper and middle class economic background prefer private OPD where as some women from middle and lower economic background prefer general OPD. Daily consultation is provided by gynaecologists (except on Sundays) in both the OPDs where women comes for their monthly check-ups.

Participants in the study have good representation of women belonging to different stages of pregnancy: women in their first, second and third trimester. Most of them falls within the age group 20 to 35 and all of them are married women (Table 5).The sample has women from various socioeconomic and cultural back grounds. Most of them are graduates where as some are post graduates. Professionals like doctors, engineers, and teachers were also represent the sample whereas majority of the women are home makers. Women who lack a minimum understanding of high school level English and any history of psychiatric illness were not a part of the sample.

Sample size. Number of sample is determined by subject to item ratio, this is 10:1 or less, which is an early and still prevalent rule of thumb for determining a priori sample size in standardizing a scale. According to Nunnally (1967), while developing an instrument, as a rule of thumb the sample size should have to be "5 to 10 times as many subjects as item" (p.322). There for the present study requires between 165 – 310 subjects for 31 items (after assessing CVI) in the newly developed PPNMS scale. The anticipated sample size is approximately 350 subjects where as 356 valid cases are finally considered for the study to ensure adequacy of the data for statistical analysis required for exploring the factor structure of the scale.

Procedure. The test package was administered directly by the researcher to each participant in the general and private OPDs at St. Stephen's and Tirath Ram Shah Hospital. Each participant who was initially screened for their age and trimester were briefed about the purpose of the research and asked for their willingness to participate in the study through a consent form.

The researcher had administered the test package individually to each participant. Those who had expressed their willingness to participate in the study were asked to sign the consent form followed by a form to furnish their demographic details and the three self report inventories consisting of the newly developed scale, 10-item PSS and WHO (five) wellbeing index.

The participants were asked to clarify their doubts if any, while responding to the test package. The entire test package could be completed approximately in 15 -20 mints and was done in the presence of the researcher, away from family and spouse either in the waiting room or in a separate room arranged by the hospital authorities as per the availability.

Preliminary tryout/ pilot test. The newly developed measure having 31 items were initially administered to a small sample of 48 pregnant women with the objective of determining the reliability, feasibility and practicality of the new measure. The questionnaire was administered with a brief instruction: both oral and written. At the end, respondents were also asked to report any ambiguity in the wordings of any of the items. The items were presented in a random order with no dimensional labels.

Since there were no ambiguity reported for any of the item and the overall response rate for the scale and for each item was above 95%, the 31 item scale was finally considered for field testing without further modifications.

Instruments used. Each subject were received a six page questionnaire booklet. The test booklet contains 5 different sections. The first section consists of general information about different sections and informed consent form, asking individual's written consent to participate in the study.

Second page consist of information regarding demographic variables such as age, marital status, occupation, education, socio-economic status specific information such as obstetric history, parity and term of gestation. The next section contains the newly developed 31 item prenatal maternal stress measure along with the instructions to respondents. The succeeding sections include Perceived Stress Scale (PSS), 10 item version (Cohen, 1983) and WHO (Five) Well-Being Index (1998 version). (The complete test booklet is given in Appendix 2)

PSS- 10 item. PSS is a global measure of perceived stress developed by Cohen in 1983. PSS was originally developed as a 14-item scale that assesses perception of stressful experiences by asking the respondents to rate the frequency of his/her feelings and thoughts related to situations that occurred over the previous month. Two shorter versions were developed latter: the PSS-4 and PSS-10 with 4 and 10 items respectively (Cohen, Kamarck, & Mermelstein, 1983).The PSS was designed for use with those at least a junior high school education. The items are easy to understand and the response alternatives are simple to grasp. Moreover, as noted above, the questions are quite general in nature and hence relatively free of content specific items. So far, the scale has been translated in many languages such as Arabic, Swedish, Spanish, Chinese, Japanese and Turkish.

Ten item PSS is the best currently available instrument with excellent reliability data among pregnant population and has high validity data in non-pregnant samples. The PSS-10 was found to have adequate reliability and validity and a slightly higher internal reliability than PSS-14 (Alpha coefficient of 0.78 vs. 0.75). Exploratory factor analysis of PSS-10 uncovered the same two- factor structure. The first factor included questions reflecting negative feelings (being upset, angry, or nervous) and inability to handle stress while the second factor included questions expressing positive emotions and ability to act in stressful situations.

Each item were rated on a five point Likert-type scale (0 = never to 4 = very often). Total scores are calculated after reversing positive item's (4, 5, 7, & 8) scores and then summing up all scores. Score ranges from 0-40. A higher score indicates more stress. Among general population, scores around 13 are considered average and high stress groups usually have a stress score of around 20 points. Scores of 20 or higher are considered high stress and needs to adopt new stress reduction techniques. This has been confirmed in more than one study that examined psychometrics of self-administered PSS-10 among different population (Cohen, 1998). The mean score on PSS- 10 among pregnant women ranges from 13-18 as reported in various studies (Wang & Chen, 2005). A distinction has also made between multipara and primipara: among primipara the mean score across studies is 16.94, $\pm$4.84 and among multipara the mean score is 19.81 $\pm$3.98 (Wang & Chen, 2005).

PSS-10 has high reliability, Cronbach's alpha between 0.84 - 0.86 and test-retest reliability 0.85. Correlation of the PSS to other measures of similar symptoms ranges between .52 - .76 (Cohen et al., 1983). Notably, high PSS scores have been correlated with higher biomarkers of stress, such as cortisol (Hilmert, Schetter, Dominguez, Abdou, Hobel, Glynn & Sandman, 2008).

WHO (five) well-being index. World Health Organization -5 Well-Being Index (WHO -5) (WHO 1998), is used to evaluate well-being in general populations and in patient population. The first version having 28 items, were reduced to 10 item following a study on alternative therapies for diabetes patients by Bech et al. (1996). These 10 items were reduced to 5 further and the 5-item version was used to screen depression in general population (WHO, 1998).

WHO (five) could be completed in only 1-2 minutes and is available in different languages (WHO: CCMH, 1998). It consists of 5 positively worded items about the respondent's feelings during the preceding 2-week period. A 6-point Likert type scale was used to rate each item from 0-5; with 0 indicating a lack of positive feelings and 5 indicating consistent positive feelings. The raw scores are transformed into a scale ranging from 0 to 100. Scores $\leq$ 50 are indicative of a poor emotional state and the need for further testing.

Validity and reliability of WHO-5 in the general population, the elderly (aged > 50 years) and individuals presenting to primary healthcare centres has been examined and confirmed. A study conducted in the Asian context to assess wellbeing of prenatal women using WHO-5 items has reported a Cronbach's alpha coefficient of 0.85. Exploratory factor analysis yielded 1 factor with an eigen value equal to 3.15, which explained 63.1% of the total variance. Confirmatory factor analysis confirmed the 1-factor structure and a WHO-5 cut-off score of < 50 exhibited optimal sensitivity for identifying psychological symptoms among prenatal women (Mortazavi, Mousavi, Chaman & Khosravi, 2015).

Statistical tools used in the study.

Descriptive statistics. The nature of the distribution was assessed initially to determine normalcy of the obtained scores using One-Sample Kolmogorov-Smirnov test in IBM SPSS Statistics version 20 and by using histograms. Prior to conducting the Exploratory Factor Analyses (EFAs), Kaiser-Meyer-Olkin (KMO) measure of sampling adequacy was used to evaluate the factorability of the data. The KMO was found to be .74, which is higher than the value (0.60) recommended by Tabachnick and Fidell (2001).

Descriptive statistic such as mean, standard deviation and range provides information on the representation of test scores on the newly developed prenatal stress scale, PSS and WHO (five) Well-being. Frequency of endorsement and homogeneity of items were inspected for the new measure. Total item correlation was assessed to determine items with lower item total correlation (<.02).

Reliability. Internal consistency reliability of the scale was assessed using Cronbach's alpha, one of the best and widely practiced measure of internal consistency. It is considered to be a measure of scale reliability which correlates how closely the items are related to each other as a group. Usually alpha should be equal to or greater than 0.8; however, a value of alpha 0.7 is also acceptable. An alpha value of .8 or less indicate the possibility of having sub dimensions for a scale

Validity. Validating a scale is a process whereby determining the degree of confidence one could place on inferences made about the scores of samples on that scale. Different forms of validity were examined in the process of validating the new scale.

Concurrent validity. In concurrent validity new measure is correlated with a previously well-established measure of that construct. In this study Cohen's PSS-10 item version, this is a widely used measure to assess perceived stress. Pearson correlation coefficient is used to examine the relationship between the new scale and PSS-10.

Divergent validity. Campbell and Fiske (1959) introduced the concept of discriminant or divergent validity for evaluating test validity. They stressed the importance of using both discriminant and convergent validity techniques while validating a new tests. A successful evaluation of discriminant validity shows that a test of concept is not highly correlated with other tests designed to measure theoretically different concepts. Hence the new measure of PNMS is expected to have a negative correlate with WHO-5 wellbeing scale, an established measure of wellbeing.

Construct validity. Construct validity refers to a scale's ability to measure the target concept and/or conceptual structure. Factor analysis is the commonly used method for evaluating construct validity. Construct validity assess both the theory behind the scale as well as the scale structure.

This was done by exploring the factorial composition using EFA for structural validity. This was further confirmed by Confirmatory Factor Analysis (CFA), that is the extent to which a scale's internal structure (inter item correlations) parallels the external structure of the target.

Exploratory factor analysis. Exploratory Factor Analysis (EFA) is a complex multistep process and a widely used statistical technique for a variety of application including scale development. Principle component analysis (PCA) with varimax rotation is the most popular method for data analysis since PCA is a quicker and cheaper alternative to factor analysis. component analysis though being one of the most popular and quicker analysis, factor analysis is preferred to component analysis since the latter is only a data reduction method and it is computed without any regard to the underlying structure caused by latent variables. If the assumption of multivariate normality is "severely violated", PAF is the most recommended method in SPSS.

While coming to the number of factors retained, Kaiser criterion of retaining all factors with eigen values greater than one is accepted as default in most statistical packages. However there is a broad consensus that this method is the least accurate for selecting the number of factors to retain, hence the study had considered scree test as an alternative while determining the number of factors to be retained in addition to considering eigen values of the factor. A scree plot is a graph of eigen values where the researcher looks for the natural bends or break points in the data and consider the data points above the break as the number of factors to retain.

Confirmatory factor analysis. Confirmatory factor analysis was carried out to determine the best fit model for PNMS and the conformity to the underlying structure of the measure explored by EFA. This was done by considering various indices of factor structure congruence and model fit such as CFI and RMSEA. Comparative fit indexes (CFI) in structural models range from 0 to 1, with larger values indicating better fit. CFI is a goodness of fit indices, which is widely used as an independent evaluation criteria and which could be used for generalizing across different sample.

Results of these various statistical assessments and their detailed discussions were given in the chapter 4, results and discussion.

Results and Discussion

Results and Discussion

Phase 1: Development of Items and Content Validity Assessment by Subject Matter Experts

Demographic details of the sample considered in the phase one is given in Table 2. The sample include women from diverse socioeconomic background, parity and trimester. The interviews conducted in phase one were centred on narrating women's unique experiences, changing perceptions about their body, changes in their life, changing relations with their partner and others including friends and relatives. Other concerns expressed by pregnant women during the interview are: approach of their spouse to their pregnancy, poor social support, economic concerns, unexpected pregnancies, changes in the body image, sleeplessness, weight gain, changing roles and responsibility, dependency, anxiety about labour and delivery, mood swings etc. Their concerns about baby, baby-care, changing roles and responsibilities, their physical constrains and emotional instabilities during this period were also discussed in great detail (Table 3).

Table 2

Demographic details of the sample interviewed in the Phase one (N=25)

Variable		Percentage	
Age	23 -35		*27.44
Gravidity	Primigravida	76	
	Multigravida	24	
Trimester	1st Trimester	12	
	2nd Trimester	44	
	3rd Trimester	44	
Economic status	Lower	24	
	Middle	48	
	Upper	28	

Note: Table showing the percentage of distribution of pregnant women in different demographic variables.

*Mean age of the sample.

DEVELOPMENT OF PREGNANCY STRESS SCALE

Table 3

Dimension	Sub dimension/Themes /Categories	Keywords/Codes
Interpersonal relation	Intimate partner	Care, Support, attentive, positive discussions about baby, insensitive, understanding
	Social support	Care, support, mother, helping, sharing information and experience, attentive, motivating, distraction, Family, friends, away from family.
Intrapersonal relations.	Fear, anxiety, preconceptions nger, Low self-esteem	Confusion, pessimism, dilemmas, taking responsibility, ambivalence, shame, changing roles and relation, tension, irritability, being unattractive, painful, inhibition, being burden, being sensitive, mood swings
Pregnancy specific concerns	planning and preparedness,	Inappropriate, awaiting, ambivalence, most wanted, financial constraints, settled in life, matured for parenting, financially secure.
	Physical concerns	Insomnia nausea, vomiting, back ache, swelling, frequently exhaustive, appetite, gaining weight, changing body image, restricted motion, low self-esteem, sleeplessness, difficulty to breath, medical risks.
	Labour and delivery	Fear, pain, unfamiliar faces, losing control, Caesarean delivery, being unconscious, feeding baby, handling baby
Concerns about baby	Concerns about Baby	Gender, having a male child,Health, Baby care, emotional attachment, appearance.
Economic concerns	Career tensions	Compromises, growth, regret, opportunities, secure, maternity leave.
	Economic instability	medical expenses, affordable, support, financially dependent, not settled,

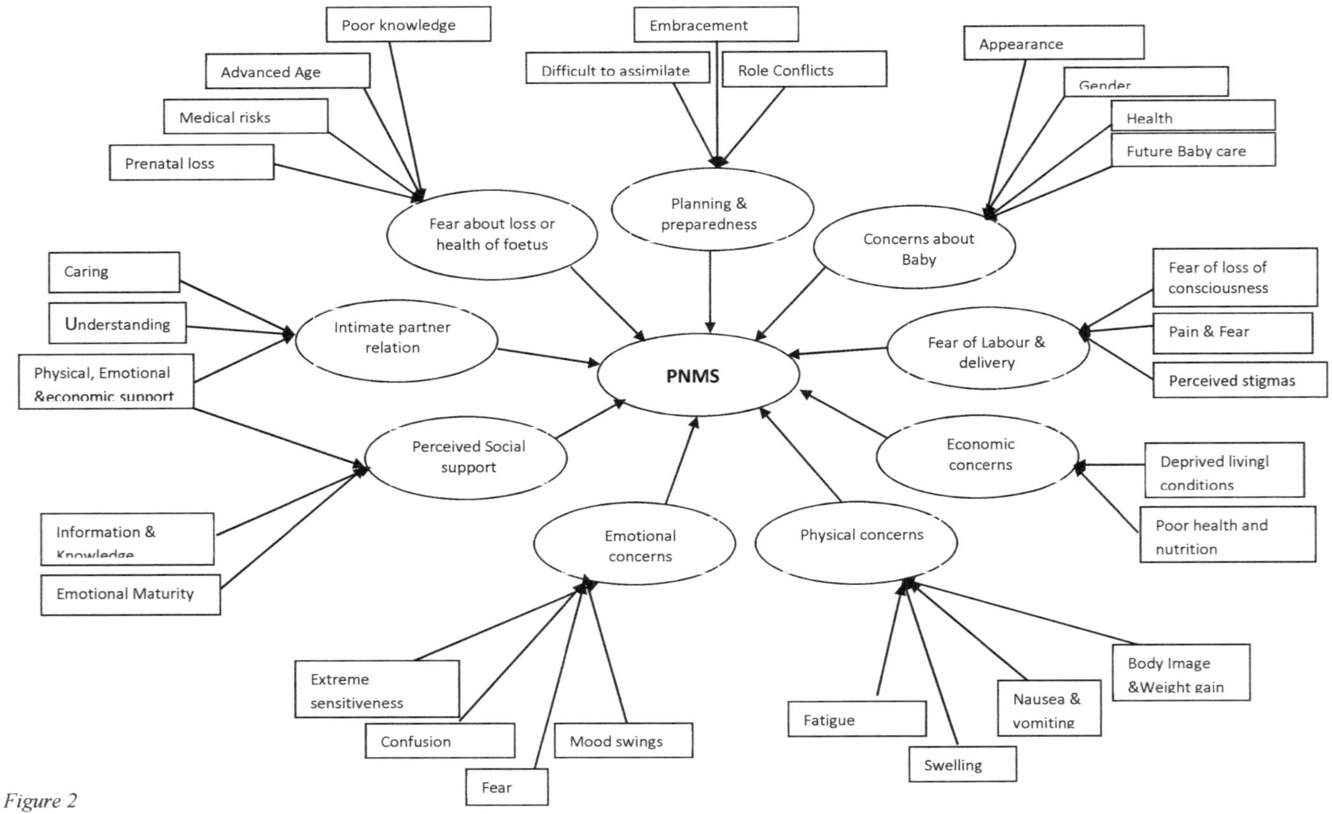

DEVELOPMENT OF PREGNANCY STRESS SCALE

Figure 2
Thematic Map depicting the themes and meaning identified from the Data

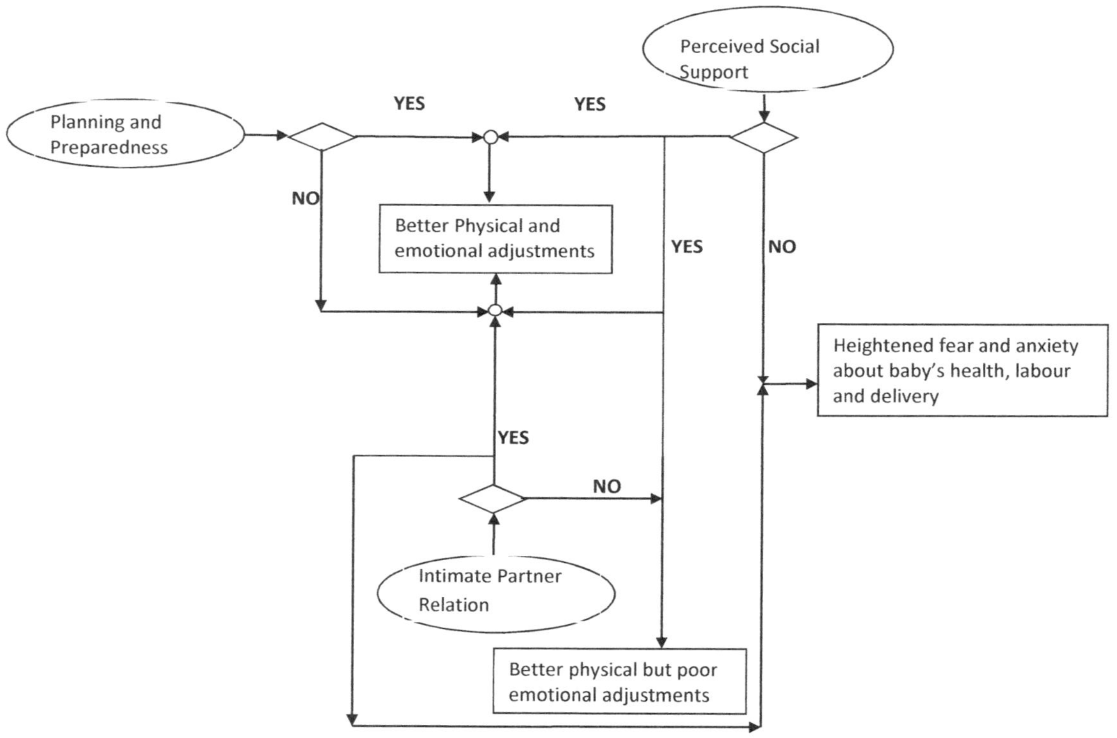

Figure 3

Flow chart depicting pattern of association among themes as identified from the data set.

DEVELOPMENT OF PREGNANCY STRESS SCALE

Table 4

I-CVI and CVR for initial 40 items

Item	N_e	I-CVI	CVR	Interpretation
I am happy about my husband's (partner's) care and attention to our pregnancy.	23	1	1	retained
I am worried about labour and delivery.	23	1	1	retained
I am hardly planned or prepared for this pregnancy and it bothers me.	19	.82	.65	retained
Being pregnant at this time irritates me.	18	.78	.56	retained
I am happy about my care or attention to this pregnancy.	19	.82	.65	retained
I am concerned about my physical changes or changes in body image.	20	.86	.74	retained
Being in the middle of problems.	16	.69	.39	removed
Being a financial dependent at this stage bothers me.	20	.86	.74	retained
I am Concerned about my baby's gender.	21	.91	.83	retained
I am concerned about others preferences for my Baby's gender.	20	.86	.74	retained
I am concerned over my professional compromises.	19	.82	.65	retained
I am getting annoyed or irritated.	21	.91	.83	retained
I am getting upset over trivial issues.	22	.96	.91	retained
I am upset over my strained relationship with friends or family.	21	.91	.83	retained
I am concerned over growing strains in my marital life.	21	.91	.83	retained
I am losing active life and happiness, which I could have otherwise.	19	.82	.65	retained
Things are not really going on my way and it bothers me.	18	.78	.56	retained
I'm being physically exhausted.	21	.91	.83	retained
I'm desperately in need to talk to someone.	19	.82	.65	retained
Physical symptoms of pregnancy such as nausea, vomiting, back ache and swelling bother me.	23	1	1	retaiend
I am concerned about my future baby care.	23	1	1	retained
I am concerned about others attitude to this pregnancy.	19	.82	.65	retained
I have disturbing thoughts about baby's health or appearance	23	1	1	retained
I am concerned that having a new baby will alter my existing relationships.	22	.95	.91	retained
I am bothered about my health compromising behaviours	20	.87	.73	retained
I often feel the need to escape from reality.	18	.78	.56	retained
I often have trouble falling asleep.	21	.91	.83	retained

DEVELOPMENT OF PREGNANCY STRESS SCALE

I often feel my life is so colourless.	19	.82	.65	retained
I am concerned about the risks of my adverse medical conditions on this pregnancy	22	.95	.91	retained
I feel I need some outlet	18	.78	.56	retained
I can't stop worrying.	18	.78	.56	retained
I am concerned over my economic conditions.	20	.87	.73	retained
My medical expenses are a matter of concern at this stage.	20	.87	.73	retained
Need to convince others on how much I value this pregnancy	14	.61	.21	removed
Have no idea about what is happening to me	13	.56	.13	removed
I am worried about handling the infant when I first come home from the hospital.	12	.52	.04	removed
Emotional ups and downs during pregnancy annoy me.	14	.60	.21	removed
The possibility of premature childbirth frightens me.	14	.60	.21	removed
I am worried that I might not become emotionally attached to the infant.	18	.78	.56	removed
I am concerned about my growing responsibilities.	12	.52	.04	removed

A total of 40 items were developed to cover these broad areas of concerns expressed by pregnant women on their intrapersonal relations, interpersonal relations, pregnancy specific concerns, concerns about baby and economic concerns (Figure 2). Items were cross examined with various standardized measures including general stress scales and pregnancy specific stress scales for any missing concerns to ensure the comprehensibility of new scale.

The items were worded in such a way that it could efficiently capture the stressor, perception of theses stressors and emotional response to them. Hence the scale adopts a multidimensional approach to PNMS consisting of: stressor, perception and emotional response as suggested by Lobel (1994), ideal for a stress measure (Figure 3).

The scale includes both negatively and positively worded items. To reduce the threats of individual response to validity, due to random or inattentive response, first person reference was interspersed in almost all the items, asking participants to select the most appropriate response (e.g. 'I am concerned....' or 'I often feel...') (Appendix 1).

Results of CVR and I-CVI of the initial pool of 40 items as assessed by 23 SMEs are given in Table 4. CVR of items ranges from 1 to 0.04; seven items has got a CVR below 0.39 (the critical value). These seven items were removed. Further two more items such as:

"38. The possibility of premature childbirth frightens me.

36. I am worried that I might not become emotionally attached to the infant", which has the potential to trigger anxiety among pregnant women, in the opinion of SMEs were also removed.

I-CVI of items in the initial scale having 40 items ranges from 1 to 0.52. Content validity index of the scale (S-CVI) after removing 9 items is 0.85.The remaining 31 items have high CVR and the S-CVI (0.85) is also acceptable (Polit & Beck, 2006).

Instrument design. The resultant scale was designed with a 4-point Likert scale for the participants to make their response ranging from 0 to 3; based on their experiences in the last few weeks (Appendix 2). A response of 0 denotes "Not At All" and 3 denote "Very Much So". Hence the scale is in an ascending order from the least to the most.

The scale contains both positively and negatively worded items; items such as 7, 12 and 19 are positively worded hence to follow reverse scoring. Total score on the scale is calculated by adding the response on this 4-point Likert scale. A higher score on the scale indicates a higher level of PNMS.

Phase 2: Standardization of the Scale

The newly developed scale is retained with 31 items related to intimate partner relation, perceived social support, economic concerns, concerns about baby, pregnancy specific concerns; both physical and emotional, fear of labour and delivery and concerns due to poor planning and preparedness, after removing eight items low in CVR in the designing phase of the scale. Each of the items in the scale has to be rated in a four-point scale with response ranges from 0 to 3. Maximum possible score on the scale is 93 and the minimum is 0, with a higher score indicating higher level of PNMS. This 31 item scale is pilot tested and field tested among pregnant women, the results of the same is given here. A total of 48 pregnant women were considered in the pilot test. Demographic details of the sample are given in the table 5.

Table 5

Demographic details of the sample considered in the Phase 2: Pilot study

Variable		N	
Age	20 -35	48	27.3*
Occupation	Homemaker	33	
	Working	10	
	Ns**	5	
Gravidity	Primigravida	24	
	Multigravida	24	
Trimester	1st Trimester	12	
	2nd Trimester	22	
	3rd Trimester	14	

Note: Table showing the distribution of pregnant women in different demographic variables. *Mean age of the sample. **Not specified

Internal consistency of the scale in the pilot trial was assessed using Cronbach's alpha, and is .80 for 31 items. Since there were no ambiguity reported for any of the item and the overall response rate for the scale and for each item was above 95%, the 31 item scale was finally considered for field testing without further modifications.

Data were screened prior to all analysis. The initial dataset contained 356 pregnant women. (from the initial 364 participants eight were removed due to the incompletion of the scales).

Table 6

Demographic details of the sample considered in the Phase 2: N= 356

Variable		N
Age	22 -33 26.11*	
Gravidity	Primigravida	190
	Multigravida	166
Trimester	1st Trimester	93
	2nd Trimester	106
	3rd Trimester	157
Occupation	Homemaker	178
	Working	116
	On leave	62
Economic Status	Lower Income Category	77
	Middle Income Category	149
	High Income Category	68
	Non response	62

Note: Table showing the demographic details of the pregnant women.
*Mean age of the sample.

The mean score of the sample ($N = 356$) on the initial 31 items and other descriptive statistics at 95% confident level is shown in the Table 7.

Table 7

Descriptive Statistics of the initial 31 item scale

Descriptive	Values
Mean	29.59
Std. Error	.63
Std. Deviation	11.94
Minimum	3
Maximum	67
Range	64

Note: Mean, Standard Deviation, variance and range of initial 31 item scale.

With regards to normality, response of none of the item is skewed. No item exceeds the cut off of ± 3 for skewness and kurtosis. Item statistics is given in the Table 8. Items were further screened for their item total correlations (Table 8). Item with total item correlation, $r < 0.2$ were removed (Clark & Watson, 1995). A widely followed practice is to consider mean inter item correlation within the range of 0.15 to 0.20 for scales that measure broad characteristics and between .40 to .50 for those tapping narrow dimensions (Clark & Watson., 1995).Three items: 3, 25 and 27 having item total correlation $r < .2$; .191, .09 and .19 respectively, were removed.

No items had shown any multicollinearity or inter item correlation coefficient over 0.9. Mean and standard deviation of the scale after removing the three item (3, 25 and 27) are 27.36 and 10.46 respectively for 28 items ($N = 356$).

Table 8

Mean and item–total correlation of 31 items PNMSS (N = 356).

Item	Min	Max	Mean	Item total correlation
Item1	0	3	.85	.54
Item 2	0	3	.84	.33
Item3	**0**	**3**	**.70**	**.18**
Item4	0	3	1.22	.29
Item5	0	3	.91	.44
Item6	0	3	1.48	.23
Item8	0	3	.44	.32
Item9	0	3	.71	.44
Item 10	0	3	1.02	.45
Item 11	0	3	1.35	.38
Item12	0	3	1.45	.25
Item 13	0	3	.94	.29
Item 14	0	3	.82	.48
Item 15	0	3	1.20	.34
Item 16	0	3	.60	.30
Item 17	0	3	1.44	.25
Item 18	0	3	1.02	.39
Item 19	0	3	.81	.29
Item 20	0	3	1.24	.43
Item 21	0	3	.72	.40
Item 22	0	3	.65	.28
Item 23	0	3	1.38	.36
Item24	0	3	1.04	.52
Item 25	0	3	.91	.19
Item26	0	3	1.32	.30
Item 27	0	3	.73	.09
Item 28	0	3	.36	.44
Item29	0	3	1.00	.31
Item 30	0	3	1.16	.41
Item 31	0	3	.51	.44

Note: Item in bold; 3, 25 and27 having item total correlation < .2 were removed.

Cronbach's alpha is used to estimate reliability of the scale. Cronbach's alpha for the newly developed scale is 0.83. Nunnaly (1978) has indicated 0.7 to be an acceptable reliability coefficient and a minimum of 0.8 is considered for diagnostic reliability. No further item were removed since all the remaining 28 items were seemed to improve reliability of the scale.

Test retest reliability was also assessed on 60 pregnant women with a time gap of 4 weeks. Demographic details are given in the Table 9. Scores of these 60 samples on 31 items at two time frames were correlated to see the test retest reliability (Table 10). The results shows that the scale has good test retest reliability (coefficient of correlation >.7 on all items).

Table 9

Demographic details of the 60 samples considered for test retest reliability

Variables		N
Age	22-35	60
Occupation	House wife	44
	Working	15
Trimester	1st trimester	12
	2nd trimester	21
	3rd trimester	26

Note: Demographic details of one sample are not given due to any response.

Validity assessment. Convergent validity of the new measure was assessed by correlating the scores on 31 item with a previously well-established measure of perceived stress; PSS-10 (Cohen, 1994), which is widely used by the researchers to assess perceived stress and PNMS. Pearson correlation coefficient is used to examine the relationship between the two measures. The results indicates the existence of a strong positive correlation between PSS-10 and the new measure significant at $p < .01$ ($r=.826, n=356, p=.00$).

Table 10

Test-retest reliability statistics of 31items on 60 pregnant women

Item	r	p
Item 1	.98	.01
Item 2	.96	.01
Item 3	.92	.01
Item 4	.93	.01
Item5	.95	.01
Item6	.84	.01
Item 7	.81	.01
Item 8	.88	.01
Item 9	.92	.01
Item10	.89	.01
Item 11	.95	.01
Item 12	.74	.01
Item 13	.98	.01
Item14	.85	.01
Item 15	.83	.01
Item16	.84	.01
Item 17	.85	.01
Item 18	.89	.01
Item 19	.88	.01
Item 20	.86	.01
Item21	.96	.01
Item22	.88	.01
Item 23	.84	.01
Item 24	.83	.01
Item 25	.94	.01
Item 26	.93	.01
Item 27	.94	.01
Item 28	.92	.01
Item 29	.84	.01
Item 30	.92	.01
Item 31	.93	.01
Total	.95	.01

Divergent validity of the new measure was assessed by correlating the cores with WHO (five) well being index (1998 version). Pearson correlation coefficient shows a strong negative correlation significant at $p < .01$ level *(r = -.539, n= 356, p=.00)*.

Factor analysis. Multiple factor analysis was conducted with the objective of comparing the item loading tables and retaining the one with the "cleanest" factor structure with item loadings above .30, no or few item cross loading and no factor with fewer than 3 items. Since a factor with fewer than 3 items are generally weak and unstable where as if it is greater than 5 a strong solid factor. (Items are thoroughly screened for any cross loading. A cross loaded item is that which has a factor loading of .32 or higher on two or more factors.) In the exploratory factor analysis (EFA), varimax rotation: an orthogonal rotation, which produces factors that are uncorrelated is preferred over the oblique methods, which allows factors to correlate. However to avoid the possible loss of valuable information if the factors are correlated, oblique rotation was also conducted in the study. Since the factors are uncorrelated, orthogonal and oblique rotation produced nearly identical results.

To uncover the underlying factor structure of the new scale a series of Exploratory Factor Analysis (EFA) was conducted using SPSS (Version 20). Data were screened prior to analysis. The initial dataset contained 356 pregnant women. A pair wise removal of the cases with missing values was performed to ensure, only valid cases were considered in the analysis. Initially, Principal Axis Factoring (PAF) with varimax rotation (orthogonal) using Kaiser Normalization was conducted to explore the factor structure of the scale.

Kaiser-Meyer-Olkin (KMO) Test of sampling adequacy was performed to determine the suitability of data for Factor Analysis. The test measures sampling adequacy for each variable in the model and for the complete model (Gourounti et al., 2012). Bartlett test result was found to be statistically significant which means the structure of the scale is suitable for factor analysis (*KMO =.75*, Bartlett test result: *df = 378, p < .001)*.

Initial EFA using PAF and varimax rotation had extracted eight factors having eigen value greater than one (Figure 4).

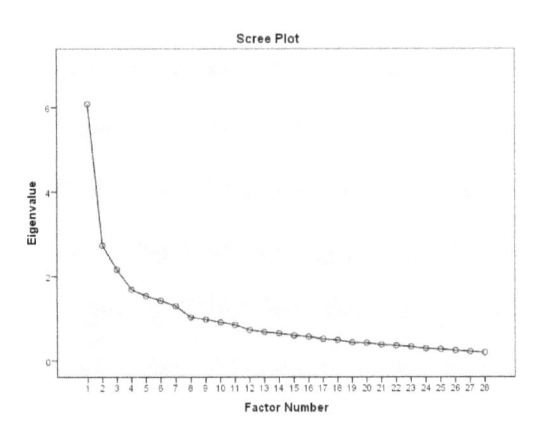

Figure 4: Scree plot of EFA using PAF (Varimax rotation) with 28 items.

A review of the scree plot for conceptual interpretability of factors (Cattell, 1966) was considered while determining the number of factors to be retained in the final scale. Out of these eight factors, three factors with less than three items were removed. Further, items which are loaded strongly (i.e., ≥ .50) but not too strongly, (i.e., ≤ .90; to avoid retaining redundant items which may create within-factor correlation measurement error) were retained for further analysis (see Table 11).

Table 11

Eigen Values of Exploratory Factor Analysis

Initial Eigen values		Extraction Sum		Rotation Sum	
Factor Total	% of variance	Total	% of variance	Total	% of variance
1. 6.01	21.7	5.60	20	3.04	10.89
2. 2.73	9.75	2.27	8	2.54	9.09
3. 2.16	7.71	1.70	6	2.24	8.00
4. 1.69	6.04	1.26	4.50	2.23	7.98
5. 1.53	5.48	1.05	3.70	1.24	4.42
6. 1.42	5.10	0.88	3.17	.95	3.50
7. 1.30	4.64	0.79	2.84	.95	3.42
8. 1.03	3.68	0.53		.87	3.12

Note: Results of Exploratory Factor Analysis using principal axis factor extraction with Varimax rotation with initial 28 items, N=356. Eigen values and percentage of variance of initial 8 factors having Eigen value >1,

A strong item retention criterion was considered to avoid retaining grammatically redundant items that create within-factor correlation measurement error. Hence items loaded under each of these five factors were thoroughly screened for any grammatical redundancy since such items in the final instrument could leads to attenuation paradox and if any such redundant item is included in the scale, the other(s) contribute virtually no incremental information. Such items will also inflate reliability (internal consistency) of the scale (Clark & Watson, 1995) without adding to its validity.

A stringent cut off >.3 was considered to improve the validity of item in the final scale. The items considered in the final scale along with their item loading are given in Table 12.

Reliability of a five factor model was further examined, since factor five have only 2 items having factor loading > .50; item 6 and 29: disturbing thoughts about baby's health or appearance and trouble falling asleep respectively. Though these items have higher loading on factor-5, statisticians recommend against retaining factors with fewer than three items (Tabachnick & Fidell, 2001). Only the initial four factors had met the item retention criterion: a loading of three or more than three items on a factor. One more item, item seven having lower factor loading on factor one, perceived social support and preparedness was removed to reduce the number of items and to retain the most valid items. Hence the final scale after initial EFA is retained with 4 factors having 15 items (Table 12).

Table 12

Factor Loadings for Exploratory Factor Analysis

Items		F1	F2	F3	F4
1.	Item 23	.708			
2.	Item 11	.684			
3.	Item 12	.645			
4.	Item 24	.551			
5.	Item 14		.723		
6.	Item 18		.592		
7.	Item 2		.533		
8.	Item 10		.511		
9.	Item 1		.502		
10.	Item 19			.814	
11.	Item 31			.681	
12.	Item 21			.656	
13.	Item 4				.77
14.	Item 16				.64
15.	Item 9				.55

Note: Results of Exploratory Factor Analysis using principal axis factor extraction with varimax rotation, $N = 356$. Items having the strongest factor loadings for each factor that met the established item retention criteria and loaded on its intended factor are given.

The first factor accounted for 21.71% of the initial variance, the second factor accounted for 9.76% of the initial variance (8.12% once extracted), the third factor accounted for 7.72% of the initial variance and the fourth factor accounted for 6.04% of the initial variance (see Table 11).

Importantly, all the four factors were conceptually interpretable. The first factor consists of items related to perceived social support and preparedness for pregnancy while the second factor consists of items related to physical and emotional concerns during pregnancy, the third factor consists of items concerning intimate partner relation and perceived stress and the fourth factor consists of items related to economic concerns.

Furthermore, an EFA using PAF extraction and quartimax rotation was conducted using these 28 items and with 15 items, results once again supporting a four-factor solution but not a five-factor solution considering the criteria of factor loading of >.5 and factors with at least three items. Hence the structure was further confirmed and the final scale is retained with 15 items under four factors (Table 13).

Table 13

Eigen Values of Exploratory Factor Analysis

Factor	Initial Eigen values Total	% of variance	Extraction Sum Total	% of variance	Rotation Sum Total	% of variance
1.	3.94	26.30	3.42	22.81	22.81	14.29
2.	2.20	14.70	1.73	11.54	11.54	13.81
3.	1.62	10.82	1.16	7.75	7.75	11.06
4.	1.47	09.80	1.02	6.80	6.80	9.73
5.	0.80	5.38				
6.	0.73	4.90				
7.	0.69	4.62				
8.	0.61	4.10				

Note: Results of Exploratory Factor Analysis using principal axis factor extraction with Quartimax rotation of 15 items having higher factor loading identified in the initial EFA, N=356. Eigen values and percentage of variance of initial 8 factors having Eigen value >1.

Follow-up model testing using confirmatory factor analysis. The next step in the process is to identify a best fit model for the construct PNMS and to compare the fit indices for a three-factor and a four factor model explored in the EFA. It is wrong to draw substantive conclusions based on exploratory analysis since by nature and design EFA is exploratory and there is no inferential statistics and it is not designed to test hypothesis or theories. Hence it is essential to move to CFA now which allows researcher to test hypothesis via inferential techniques to determine the conformity of the structure across certain population subgroups.

After examining the factor structure of the newly developed measure using EFA a series of CFAs were conducted using Amos 22.0.0 in the phase 2.

Model fit was evaluated using Comparative Fit Index (CFI), Tucker Lewis Index (TLI) and Root Mean Square Error of Approximation (Martens, 2005). CFI is a goodness of fit indices, which is among the independent evaluation criteria. CFI values range from 0 to 1, with larger values indicating better fit. As the value of goodness-of-fit indices approaches 1, the fit between the model and data increases. The comparative fit index (CFI) analyzes the model fit by examining the discrepancy between the data and the hypothesized model, while adjusting for the issues of sample size inherent in the chi-squared test of model fit and the normed fit index (Bentler, 1980).

In contrast, error indices RMSEA is acceptable when it is below 0.08, whereas values below 0.05 indicate better fit. RMSEA values in the range of .05 to .08 indicate fair fit, and that values greater than .10 indicate poor fit (Browne and Cudeck, 1993). However considered values in the range of .08 to.10 to indicate fair fit. The $\chi2/df$ ratio should be smaller than 3, whereas a value below 5 is also acceptable.

To know a best fit model for the construct, the above mentioned model fit indicators of conformity factor analysis was considered (Table 14).

Table 14

CFI, TLI and RMSEA of the two models using Confirmatory Factor Analysis

Indices	Results for the four factor model	Results for the three factor model
$\chi2/df$	4.30	4.29
CFI	.81	.88
TLI	.73	.80
RMSEA	.09	.09

Note: Results of Confirmatory Factor Analysis

Considering these conventional cut off criteria as a rule of thumb, both the models don't exhibit a great fit indices; however the fit indices, CFI is closer to 0.9, (0.88) for the three factor model which is better than .81of the four factor model. In addition, all the items have a higher factor loading on the corresponding factor. Therefore, it was concluded that both the models have a fair fit and the three-factor model have a better fit as compared to the four-factor model. However in future research, it is recommended to use 15 items, four factor scale since the 3-factor model being much condensed version and will lacks the multidimensionality of the much expected stress measure.

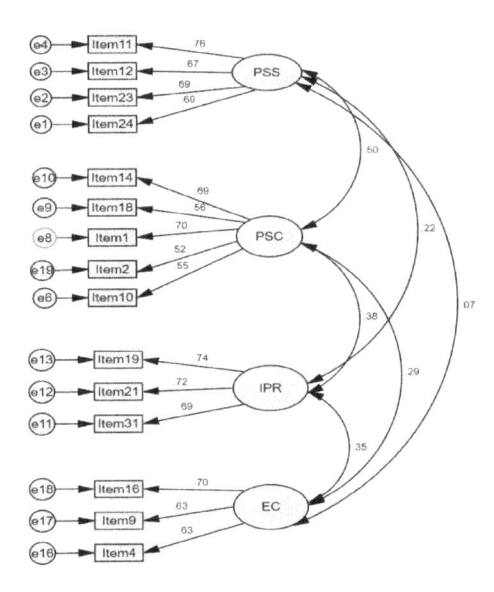

Figure 5. Four Factor structure of PPNMS scale using CFA

Note: Item loading of each of the item on the corresponding factor is displayed. PSS denotes Perceived Social Support and Preparedness (Factor 1), PSC denotes Pregnancy Specific Concerns (factor 2), IPR denotes Intimate Partner Relations (Factor 3) and EC denotes Economic concerns (Factor 4).

In summary, the four-factor solution having 15 items seems to offer a best fit structure for the scale and an efficient model to assess PNMS comprehensively. Cronbach's alpha of all the four factors except Economic concerns (.69) is above .7 which is considered as statistically acceptable reliability coefficient (Nunnaly, 1978).

Factor Description and discussion

To determine the reliability of each of these subscales that constitute the latent construct PNMS, internal consistency of these four subscales were assessed using Cronbach's alpha. The first factor, perceived social support and preparedness having items: 11, 23, 12 and 24 have a Cronbach's alpha .77 and all the items contribute to improve the internal consistency reliability of the factorial composition. This suggests that all the items considered under the factor are valid and it measures the same latent construct, perceived social support and preparedness. Further, a strong correlation of items related to one's planning and preparedness to pregnancy with items indented to capture perceived social support of pregnant women may suggests that perceived social support prepares a women to pregnancy and there by reduces the worries and concerns associated with it.

A paired sample T-test was did by correlating the scores on the individual scale with the total score. It has found that the scores on these four subscales are significantly correlated with the total scale, indicating that each of these four factors are major constituents of the construct, PNMS. It has also found that scores on the sub scale, pregnancy specific stress, both emotional and physical concerns have a higher positive correlation ($r = .77, p < .00$) as compared to other sub scales.

A strong positive correlation of total score with the subscale perceived social support and preparedness ($r = .67, p < .00$) is in consistent with previous studies which indicates, social support prepares women to adapt to new roles and to be more responsive to the baby and it also facilitate their intimate relationship (Baker & Taylor, 1997) and absence of this may contributes to prenatal stress significantly. Studies also suggest that lack of social support may leads to depression among women and would negatively affect the health of the baby (Hung, 2007). Hence social support is an important component which prepares the pregnant women to accept the challenges of being pregnant and to adapt to the new roles without any internal conflict.

Table 15

Mean, Standard Deviation of the four sub groups on the sub dimension, Perceived Social Support and Preparedness

Variables	N	Mean	Min	Max	SD
Home Maker	178	5.15	0	11	2.58
Working	116	5.30	0	11	2.93
Primigravida	189	5.4	0	11	2.76
MultiGravida	166	4.87	0	11	2.71
Total	356	5.15	0	11	2.75

Note: Mean, Standard Deviation and other descriptive of the four sub groups of the sample on the dimensions, Perceived Social Support.

Table 16

Mean, Standard Deviation of the four sub groups on the sub dimension, Pregnancy Specific Concerns

Variables	N	Mean	Min	Max	St. dev
Home Maker	178	4.44	0	12	2.98
Working	116	4.46	0	12	3.34
Primigravida	189	4.69	0	12	3.10
MultiGravida	166	4.13	0	12	3.00
Total	356	4.42	0	12	3.06

Note: Mean, Standard Deviation and other descriptive of the four sub groups of the sample on the dimensions, Pregnancy Specific concerns.

The second factor, physical and emotional concerns of pregnancy, a more pregnancy specific concern having items 18, 2, 1, 10 and 14 has a Cronbach's alpha .74 and all the items contributes to improve the internal consistency of the factor. In the confirmatory factor analysis the correlation between latent variable: perceives social support and pregnancy specific concern is .5, though moderate, this is higher that correlation with other latent variables (Figure 5). This shows the possibility of an influence of perceived social support on perceived concerns related to pregnancy, which is in conformity with previous studies (Hung, 2007). Hence the results shows that though pregnancy specific concerns and perceived social support are two distinct and independent factors, perceived social support helps in reducing pregnancy specific concerns.

A comparative study conducted among two groups of pregnant women with and without social support has found that frequency of low birth weight infants are less in the group having high social support (Hung, 2007).

Role of social support has also given significance in the culture. This leads to the practice of organizing various culture specific gatherings during the time of pregnancy. Henshaw (2003) suggests that social gatherings and ceremonies as a part of custom and tradition will help to improve women's perception of positive social support and has to be followed. Studies also show that social rituals during pregnancy as well as after delivery in the Asian culture had helped to reduce postpartum depression among Asian women (Stern & Krukman, 1983).

Table 17

Mean, Standard Deviation of the four sub groups on the sub dimension, Intimate Partner Relation

Variable	N	Mean	Min	Max	SD
Home Maker	178	1.80	0	9	.82
Working	116	2.17	0	9	.26
Primigravida	189	1.99	0	9	1.98
MultiGravida	166	1.95	0	9	1.99
Total	356	1.98	0	9	.98

Note: Mean, Standard Deviation and other descriptive of the four sub groups of the sample on the dimensions, Intimate Partner Relation.

Cronbach's alpha of the third factor, intimate partner support and perceived stress, having items 19, 21 and 31 is .76 and all the items contributes to improve the reliability of the factorial composition. This findings are in conformity with the earlier studies which shows, women who are nurtured by her male partner reports less emotional and physical symptoms, labour and child birth complications and easier postpartum adjustments (Aarts, Vingerhoets, 1993; Reece, 1993). Hence, an indifferent approach from the partner during pregnancy could positively contribute to PNMS.

Finally the fourth factor, economic concerns consisting of items 4, 16 and 9 have a Cronbach's alpha .69 and all the items contributes to improves the internal consistency of the factor structure.

Table 18

Mean, Standard Deviation of the four sub groups on the sub dimension Economic Concerns

Variable	N	Mean	Min	Max	SD
Home Maker	178	2.57	0	9	1.97
Working	116	2.21	0	9	2.32
Primigravida	189	2.58	0	9	2.43
MultiGravida	166	2.31	0	9	2.37
Total	356	2.44	0	9	2.40

Note: Mean, Standard Deviation and other descriptive of the four sub groups of the sample on the dimensions, Economic Concerns.

Mean and Standard deviation of these 15 items and four factors are given in the (Table 19). Mean scores on the entire scale and it's four dimensions for women belonging to different parity (primigravidas and multigravidas) and employment status (home makers and employed) were assessed for the purpose of comparing each sub groups with the entire scale as well as on the four dimensions of the scale.

Table 19

Mean, Standard Deviation of the sample on four sub dimensions, entire scale and the four sub groups

Factors	N	Mean	Min	Max	SD
Perceived Social support*	356	5.15	0	11	2.75
Pregnancy Specific Concerns*	356	4.42	0	12	3.06
Intimate Partner Relations*	356	1.98	0	9	1.98
Economic Concerns*	356	2.44	0	9	2.40
Scale Score*	356	14.00	1	35	6.62
House Wives	168	14.42	1	29	6.20
Working	116	14.11	0	35	7.35
Primigravidae	189	14.68	1	35	6.79
Multigravida	166	13.27	1	34	6.35

Note: Mean, Standard Deviation and other descriptive of the sample on the entire scale and it's four sub dimensions.

A further analysis into the mean scores of primigravidas and multigravidas on the entire scale has found a significant differences between the two groups ($p < .05$). It has also found that the primigravidas has a higher mean score on the scale (+ 0.63) as compared to the score of the entire sample at the same time multigravida has a mean score on the scale which is lower than (-0.73) the sample mean. The results are in conformity with the earlier studies which associate a significant level of maternal anxiety among primigravida (Wing Cheung, Yim & Dominic Chan, 2006) as compared to multigravida.

In a study conducted by Waters and colleagues (1999) among 31 pregnant women had suggests that multigravidas are more confident about their pregnancy, less fatigue and less sleep deprived as compared to primigravidas. However they had failed to identify any significant difference between these two groups. Hence a further enquiry has made to identify any significant variations among these two groups on the 4 sub scales of PPNMSS. But it has found that the groups have no significant difference on any of these dimensions, though the primigravidas has a higher mean score on all the subscales as compared to the multigravidas and 20% of primigravidas have a score >8 on the pregnancy specific concerns *(Mean* = 4.42) where as this is only 13% among multigravidas. This suggests many primigravidae have higher pregnancy specific concerns as compared to the multigravidas. This could be mainly attributed to lack of knowledge and experiences about pregnancy which could be very well addressed through good social support. Which is very much evident in the results of factor loading which shows perceived social support is well correlated with less stress from planning and preparedness to pregnancy, since the social support aids the women to be well prepared for her pregnancy.

But the results failed to show any significant difference in pregnancy specific stress among primigravida and multigravidae mainly due to the diverse nature of the sample, considered mainly for exploring he factor structure as well as limitations in sample size.

On the subscale, perceived social support and preparedness, while comparing with the mean score of the sample (*Mean* = 5.15), primigravidae has higher mean score (+.25) than multigravidae (-.28). This suggests, primigravidae has lower level of perceived social support as compared to the multigravidae, this could be the reason for the mean variations in the perceived stress between primigravidae and multigravidae.

A further enquiry into the percentage of women belonging to higher stress brackets under each group has found that 51% of primigravidas have a score >6 on the subscale perceived social support and preparedness, where as only 44% of multigravidae falls within this level. The findings are in consistent with the study conducted by Bester and Nolte (2000) on the knowledge and expectation of childbirth among primigravidae, they had identified a larger gap exists in the primigravidae's preparation to childbirth. Hence knowledge and experience about child birth leads to less stress on planning and preparedness among multigravidae as compared to primigravidae, but if primigravidae has good perceived social support, their perceived stress from poor planning and preparedness could be reduced due to better knowledge about pregnancy acquired through social support.

Interestingly there is no significant difference on prenatal maternal stress among working and housewives on the entire scale as well as on any of these four dimensions. However there is a notable difference on the scores of economic concerns among working and nonworking pregnant women. Though the group differences is not significant, the scores of economic concerns (*Mean score* = 2.44), in a range of 0 to 9, only 46% of working women has a score >2 where as 70% of housewives have a score > 2 on economic concerns (Table 18). This suggests that as compared to working pregnant women a higher percentage of housewives have perceived stress on financial concerns.

With four meaningful factors explored in the factor analysis, factor structure of the scale and the pattern of stress among each group of pregnant women belonging to different demographic variables are in greater conformity with the existing literature.

Summary and Conclusion

Summary and Conclusion

The purpose of the investigation is to develop a multidimensional instrument to assess PNMS comprehensively. Though some measures had considered the underlying factors explored in the early studies such as physical concerns during pregnancy, perceived social support, intimate partner relations, fear of delivery as independent latent variables, it is essential to understand that they all have an equally important role in predicting the latent construct, PNMS. Hence any measure which intends to assess PNMS should have this comprehensive view about the construct. This supports the approach adopted in this study in identifying the stable latent dimensions which are the constituents of PNMS. The strength of the scale has to be viewed in the background of the absence of a multidimensional, comprehensive scale having strong psychometric properties.

The initial scale having 31 items have good scale content validity as assessed by subject matter experts, which suggest that all the items in the scale efficiently assess the construct PNMS. The scale has a diagnosable reliability and good convergent and divergent validity with concurrent scales.

In consistent with the previous research, the new scale established a close parallel with perceived stress, at the same time a negative relationship with wellbeing index. A strong negative correlation of the new measure with the measure of wellbeing indicates the potential threat to the health and wellbeing of prenatally stressed women. This suggests, a higher level of PNMS compromises the wellbeing of pregnant women and such a condition is considered as a great risk for the growth and development of the foetus.

The series of EFA supports a four factor structure for the scale with 15 items having a strong loading on perceived social support and preparedness, pregnancy specific concerns: emotional and physical concerns, intimate partner relations and economic concerns. A strong correlation of items which assess preparedness with perceived social support suggests that social supports prepares a women for her pregnancy by reducing her fear about delivery and various concerns during pregnancy, especially among primigravidae. Hence a low score on this scale indicate the women have higher perceived social support and she is better prepared for pregnancy, where as a higher score indicates lower level of perceived social support.

An in depth analysis into the scores has found that the scores on the entire scale (15 items) is significantly correlated with the subscale perceived social support and preparedness. This is in consistent with previous studies which suggest that poor support could lead to stress and trauma which is a potential risk for both the mother and the baby. Hence social support is considered as a better coping strategy perceived by women, which helps her to face adverse circumstances during pregnancy. This further emphasises the cultural importance given to social gatherings and celebrations associated with pregnancy, since it improves her perceived social support.

A significant correlation of intimate partner support with the total score, PNMS suggests that poor support of the intimate partner could leads to higher level of PNMS among women. This is in conformity with the previous studies which states women who have better relation with intimate partner or those who are satisfied in their relation with intimate partner have better quality of life and wellbeing despite of their economic status. Hence, an indifferent approach from the partner during pregnancy could positively contribute to PNMS.

Overall, the scores on the four dimensions that constitute PNMS are significantly correlated with the total scores on the scale. Though each of the subscales on the newly developed measure has statistically acceptable level of internal consistency reliability the entire scale or total score has a higher, diagnosable reliability. This suggests that while looking at the total score it is also essential to look into each dimension to identify the potential source of stressor.

Finally, while comparing the reliability of the two possible models of PNMS, consisting of 15 item under 4-factors such as: perceived social support, pregnancy specific concerns, intimate partner relations and economic concerns with 3-factor model consisting of only the first three factors having 10 items in total; the four factor model has found to be more reliable as compared to a the other considering the purpose of such a comprehensive scale.

Limitations of the Present Study and Suggestions for Future Research

Though construct, concurrent and divergent validity is examined in the study using a diverse sample of different parity and gravidity, it is also desirable to further examine the cross-cultural reliability and validity of the scale among diverse groups (e.g., race/ethnicity and geographic location).

Predictive validity is not evaluated in the present study, hence it is recommended to assess the predictive validity of the scale by conducting a longitudinal study on pregnant women. Such studies should focus more on correlating the scores of the scale with the pregnancy outcome.

Since the participants were initially informed that the questions are intended to assess prenatal stress participants could have self-selected to be a part of the study based on their interest in the topic and comfort. Hence those who chose not to participate may be different than those who did.

Finally the study has identified the scores of housewives on economic concerns is higher than working pregnant women which requires further investigation in the future studies and this is not further enquired in the present study, since it is outside its scope.

Implications for Future Research

Being a comprehensive multidimensional scale having diagnosable reliability, practitioners could relay on the scores of the new measure to assess PNMS and to extend support to pregnant women who is having potentially higher score on the scale and any of its sub scales.

Earlier studies indicate that prenatal stress is an intrauterine risk for preterm birth and babies with low birth weight. Foetal programming hypothesis also supports this, by stating that prolonged exposure to PNMS results in foetal level of cortisol reflecting that of the maternal level and this potentially affects the growth and development of the foetus. Hence, an early detection of prenatal stress and timely intervention to saves the mother and the child from potential risks is at most required.

Since researchers and health care professionals are handicapped due to the absence of a multidimensional scale which assesses PNMS comprehensively and general stress measures are not as efficient as pregnancy specific stress measure to assess PNMS; this requires them to use a number of general and pregnancy specific stress measures which is often cumbersome and time consuming. Being a multidimensional, comprehensive scale having good psychometric properties, the present scale is highly relevant in this context. Hence the new measure will help the researchers to arrive at a more predictive outcome by enhancing the reliability of such studies.

Being a very brief scale having just 15 items, with good content validity and diagnosable reliability, the scale is neither context specific nor limited to any particular aspect of prenatal stress. The scores on it's sub scales such as perceived social support and preparedness, pregnancy specific concerns, intimate partner relations and economic concerns helps to identify on which dimension the women is having a higher level of stress and to develop an intervention which is tailor made to address the specific issues and concerns during her pregnancy.

A wide use of the scale as a screening tool during the monthly check ups will help to remove the stereotype associated with prenatal counselling and to consider it as a part of the regular health care system. It also helps to provide timely assistance to those women who are at risk, which will considerably improve their health and wellbeing.

Conclusion

Results from the two phases of this investigation have provided initial support for reliability and validity of the scale when used with pregnant women. The ability of the new measure to assess PNMS comprehensively can facilitate more insight into the variations in the pattern of PNMS among different sections of population through future research.

The utility of the progressive 4-factor model of PNMS is that it consists of most valid components such as perceived social support and preparedness, pregnancy specific concerns: both physical and emotional, intimate partner relations and economic concerns that assess perceived stress among pregnant women more comprehensively. This self report inventory could be completed in less than 10 minute and has good psychometric properties, hence provides the most valid scores on PNMS.

Since stress, depression and anxiety is as high as 15% among pregnant women (O'Hara & Swaim, 1996), the scale facilitates future research in this topic and will aids in prevention and timely interventions to improves the health and wellbeing among pregnant women by reaching out with professional psychological assistance.

CPSIA information can be obtained
at www.ICGtesting.com
Printed in the USA
BVHW041415160423
662363BV00007B/390